THE FUN FACTOR

CAROLYN GREENWICH

The McGraw-Hill Companies, Inc.

Sydney New York San Francisco Auckland
Bangkok Bogotá Caracas Hong Kong
Kuala Lumpur Lisbon London Madrid
Mexico City Milan New Delhi San Juan
Seoul Singapore Taipei Toronto

To my family,
my husband Vic, my sons Victor, Alex and Nicholas,
my parents Jacquelin and Harrison Hart
and my sister Linda Urquhart

Thank you for your love, support, encouragement and sense of fun

McGraw·Hill Australia

A Division of The *McGraw·Hill* Companies

Reprinted 1997, 1998
Text © 1997 Carolyn Greenwich
Illustrations and design © 1997 McGraw Hill Book Company Australia Pty Limited
Additional owners of copyright are named in on-page credits.

National Library of Australia Cataloguing-in-Publication data:

Greenwich, Carolyn.
The fun factor: games, sales contests and activities that make work fun and get results.

ISBN 0 07 470434 6

1. Employee motivation. I. Title.
658.314

Published in Australia by
McGraw-Hill Book Company Australia Pty Limited
4 Barcoo Street, Roseville NSW 2069, Australia
Publisher: John Rowe
Production Editors: Carol Grabham and Caroline Hunter
Designer: Todd Pierce
Cover design: Snapper Graphics
Cartoons: Greg Gaul
Typeset in 12pt Palatino
Desktopped by Eleanor Crowley
Printed in Australia by McPherson's Printing Group

Contents

Contents

Contents

Contents

How to Use this Book

Managers, team leaders and supervisors are all searching for ways to motivate their staff to achieve better sales results, create greater customer satisfaction and be more productive at work. There is an endless search to hire that ideal employee—one who will, almost magically, achieve top sales results, meet deadlines and maintain high standards at all times.

Managers quickly realize that their job is to help everyone under their guidance to be the best that they can be at work, and to continually help them to improve their performance. To do this, managers need ideas. This book offers more ways than any one manager could think of to motivate staff to achieve results, learn new skills and have fun doing it!

The Fun Factor is a collection of business games, sales contests and training activities used by many managers, trainers, supervisors and team leaders on the job, in sales meetings and in the seminar classroom. The central theme throughout this book is 'Fun'. The word 'Factor' is an acronym for the six motivational needs that the managers satisfy for the employees through these activities:

Fun
Appreciation
Competition
Team building
Optimize training
Recognition.

The activities in this book fall into at least one of these categories.

The *Fun* activities are designed mainly to boost the morale and generate a positive atmosphere in the office. All managers agree that when their staff are feeling happy, they give better customer service, generate more sales, and are more productive at work.

Appreciation is what everyone seems to crave. Being appreciated is one of the strongest motivators of employees. The 'appreciation' ideas let team members know that managers are grateful for their efforts. Staff who feel special and appreciated are more inclined to treat colleagues and customers in the same way.

Competition is a major stimulant, especially in a sales environment. A variety of ideas are given that involve individual competition, group competition, competition against personal past performance and bonus and commission ideas. The key to successful competitions is to use a variety.

Team building activities stimulate the team spirit of members of the office. Everyone likes to feel a sense of belonging and support. Many of the team activities include a competition element, others are simply ways to bring the group together.

Optimize training and the team will continually improve. These learning activities can be used 'on the job' or at sales and training meetings. Selling and customer service skills need to be continually reinforced and improved to keep the staff motivated.

Recognition is a powerful motivating force. There are many ways to give recognition for a job well done. The manager who cannot pay a commission or bonus can use other forms of recognition suggested here.

These ideas will be more useful if activities are used from each category. Select those that suit your office, retail outlet or call center, or that can be easily adapted. Many ideas have arisen from the feedback of the staff themselves, who recognize the need for external motivation. To find out what motivates the team, the best people to ask are the team members!

For easy reference, the book follows a set format. Under each activity, information is given under the following headings:

- Purpose
- Method
- Time
- Resource
- Reward/Prize/Gift/Bonus
- Benefit
- Source.

Special thanks to the managers, team leaders, consultants, trainers and speakers whose ideas for games, sales contests and activities have made this book possible. The contributor of each Fun Factor idea is named as the source. More information about the person can be found in the Contributors section at the end of the book.

I am already at work on the next edition and I would love to hear from you. What activities do you use? Please write to me or call me.

Carolyn Greenwich
Winning Attitudes
17 Bridge Street
Sydney, NSW 2000
Ph: 02 9241 1361

1

The Fun FACTOR

Fun

The 'Rev-Up' Session

Rev up your team so they'll rev up results! The staff at this bank arrive 15 minutes early so that they can get off to the right start.

Purpose

- To help put the office in an enthusiastic mood for the day
- To help employees focus on their daily goals
- To communicate new information
- To motivate employees to do their best for the day

Method

Use the first 15 minutes of each day or 15 minutes before work to have a 'Rev-Up' session. The following discussions could be on the agenda:

1. Start the session by recapping on some good news from the day before.
2. On a Monday morning, let staff members take turns to tell what happened on their weekend.
3. Praise individual and group performance.
4. Ask staff what areas they feel they could improve on that day and ask for suggestions as to how.
5. Communicate new information.
6. Announce any daily incentives or games.
7. Answer any questions or concerns the staff may have.
8. If special work is to be allocated, this is a good venue at which to do it.
9. Ask one person in the group to come up with a slogan for the day.

Time

Take 15 minutes, before or at the start of each day

Benefit

- Helps break any bad moods that could affect performance
- Encourages everyone to focus on the day ahead

SOURCE   Soula Skliros

The `Potluck` Lunch

Both an international freight company and an insurance company have great fun and success using the Potluck Lunch in their office. Staff thoroughly enjoy preparing delicious dishes for each other and showing off their cooking skills.

- To have fun and let people express themselves in a way other than by work

Method

Ask everyone to bring in their favorite dish for a potluck lunch at the office. It should be large enough for ten to fifteen portions. They may choose to make or bring in a dish that expresses something of their culture, personality or culinary talents. Have a variety of dishes, including salads, main courses and desserts. Provide non-alcoholic beverages for the lunch.

Time

Great fun, once or twice a year, for one hour

Resources

Paper plates and cups, cutlery, facilities for heating food

Benefit

- Provides a break from the routine of work
- Gives everyone something to look forward to

SOURCE   Bob Westcott; Jenni Swistak

Trainer's Notes:

The Newcomers' Morning Tea

Staff love to feel that they have personally met and talked to the top manager. The manager of this bank call center has over 300 staff. If she doesn't meet and talk to staff when they start, she could miss meeting the newcomers altogether.

Purpose

- To welcome on board new staff members during a group induction
- To allow the senior manager and the newcomers to get to know each other

Method

During the first week of training, the newcomers are invited to the senior manager's office for morning tea. This works very well in offices where there may be an intake of several people at once. If the numbers are too great, the morning tea can be held in a larger venue.

During the morning tea, the newcomers introduce themselves to each other and the manager. They are given a chance to ask any questions. It gives managers an opportunity to welcome newcomers personally, explain their personal vision and tell the group some background to their career with the company. The morning tea should be relaxed and informal.

Time

It takes just one hour on the newcomers' first day or during their first week

Resource

Tea and coffee, selection of tempting pastries or biscuits

Benefit

- Makes new people feel that the senior manager cares about them and wants to know them (the newcomers feel special and this reinforces the idea that they must make the customers feel special, too)
- Gives newcomers a chance to get to know the senior manager personally

SOURCE   Jeannine Walsh

The Stress Box

The insurance company supervisor who introduced the stress box found that it lifted morale immediately. There is almost no cost involved, because staff contribute their own candy.

Purpose

- To give an outlet for moments of stress

Method

Provide a box, jar or basket into which staff members can contribute a variety of candies.

Place the stress box near the team leader or supervisor. When people feel they need some relief from the pressure of the phone, they can stand up and walk to the stress box for a candy and a quick chat to the supervisor.

Encourage contributions to the stress box by staff. Write thank you notes or notes of acknowledgment for those who contribute.

Place these notes by the stress box for all to see.

Time

Great to use all the time, or in those stressful moments of the year

Resource

Container

Benefit

- Helps distract people in stressful moments
- Provides staff with a way of giving to others

SOURCE   Elaine Karr

Trainer's Notes:

Text © 1997 Carolyn Greenwich. Design and illustration © 1997 McGraw-Hill Book Co Australia Pty Ltd

Charity Day

Employees appreciate being given the opportunity to support a charity together. A group contribution always seems more significant than an individual contribution. This is a real 'feel good' activity that builds team spirit and helps others who are less fortunate.

Purpose

- To celebrate a day of giving and charity
- To let employees know that the business cares about helping others and not only about making a profit
- To help create a culture of caring

Method

Designate a charity for the organization to support. When the charity has a special day or awareness week of celebration and donation, provide activities that involve the staff.

Place posters and donation boxes around the room and hold team events to raise money. On the charity day, ask everyone to wear either the company T-shirt or a color that signifies the charity.

Take team photos and display these later in the staff tea room.

Time

One day or one week a year for each charity the company supports

Resource

Posters and collection boxes from the charity; raffle tickets and a prize for raising money; company T-shirts; film and camera

Benefit

- Stimulates the good feeling of helping others
- Contributes to a worthy cause
- Highlights the company's esprit de corps
- Encourages team-building activities

SOURCE   Rick Barrett

The Christmas Breakfast

This event is so popular at this bank that it has become the highlight of the year. The company mascot, a 'friendly dragon', accompanies Santa Claus to the Christmas breakfast. When it started, only the staff members' own children came, but it has grown to include grandchildren, nieces and nephews—everyone wants to be a part of it!

Purpose

• To involve children in the working life of the staff

Method

On the last working day or week before Christmas, have a special children's breakfast complete with Santa Claus and gifts for the children, grandchildren, nieces and nephews of staff.
    The breakfast can be held in the staff cafeteria. The children could be invited to visit the office during the event to see where the parent or other relative works.

Time

Lots of fun, and it takes only three hours during the week before Christmas

Resource

Venue for breakfast; Santa Claus; Christmas presents

Benefit

• Contributes to staff morale
• Shows people that the company cares about their families

SOURCE   Jeannine Walsh

People Say the Darnedest Things

Laughter is one of the best stress relievers. If you can laugh at it, you can live with it! The humor board gives everyone in the office a place on which to capture the humorous things that both staff and customers might say.

Purpose

- To add humor and levity to the day

Method

Have a special humor board and write on it some of the funny things that customers or staff say. Alternatively, put them in the newsletter. Here are some examples:

1. Customer service rep to caller: 'Do you mind if I hold you for a while?'
2. Customer leaving a message on the answer phone: 'Could you get back on top of me?'
3. Recipient of a telemarketing call: 'I don't speak to people who call me on the phone!'

You can also use the board as a place for staff to post funny jokes and cartoons that they feel will give everyone a laugh.

Time

Make the board a permanent fixture in the office

Resource

White board or large sheet of paper

Benefit

- Gives people an outlet to share and enjoy the 'darnedest things' that people say

SOURCE   Bill St James; Vicki Jeffery; Vic Greenwich

Foot-in-mouth disease

The Turkey Award

When this postal and freight company started using the Turkey Award, it was to be given every week. But staff felt that they were missing too many good opportunities to pass on the Turkey Award, so it was passed on daily or even hourly, as an event occurred that warranted this type of acknowledgment. The certificate can be awarded to the best of the 'Turkeys'.

Purpose

- To make light of our silly mistakes
- To add laughter and fun to the day

Method

The Turkey Award can be presented each hour, day or week. It goes to the lucky person who has made a blunder or said something funny without realizing it.

The Turkey Award is a ridiculous-looking symbol or trophy that sits on the recipient's desk for the specified time. This person can designate who will receive the trophy next, and why. A certificate such as the one shown on page 11 could also be presented.

This is great fun because everyone loves to suggest something silly that another person has done.

Time

An ongoing award that is passed from person to person

Resource

A ridiculous-looking object that can represent the 'Turkey Award' trophy; certificate as shown on page 11

Benefit

- Helps people to 'lighten up'

SOURCE Vicki Jeffery

Turkey Award

This magnificent award is presented to

_____

for brightening our day with the following comment

The Stress-Free Zone

The employees of the photographic company that use the Stress-Free Zone embrace the zone with great gusto. If someone arrives at work in a bad mood, their fellow staff members direct them straight to the Stress-Free Zone until they have a more positive frame of mind.

Purpose

• To have a special place where staff can go for a few moments to relieve stress

Method

Set aside a special place and collect in it a variety of stress relief aids. For example, one office has a punching bag that yells 'Hooray!' when someone hits it. In moments of stress, any person can go to the area and hit the bag. It creates a lot of laughter in the group.

The zone could also have a comfortable chair and some magazines. The stressed person may choose to sit quietly for a few minutes and read. When people see one of their team members in the Stress-Free Zone, they often tease their fellow worker into a better mood.

Time

Make this a permanent place in the office

Resource

A special place in the office with any stress relief aids the group can collect

Benefit

• Acknowledges to team members that the manager knows they do have stressful moments
• Stops a bad mood from spreading around the group
• Provides an outlet in times of stress

SOURCE   Yvonne Byrne

The **Friday** Quiz

Staff of the insurance company who use the Friday Quiz look forward to it every week. A non-work activity during a lunch hour holds great appeal. Everyone anticipates their turn at preparing the questions.

Purpose

- To have a non-work activity that adds interest to the week and gives a sense of anticipation

Method

Each week, an employee prepares a quiz of between twenty and fifty questions on a topic or topics of interest to team members. The quiz is prepared each week by a different person. It does not include product knowledge questions. Over lunch on Friday, or on a day of the week that is quiet, the quiz is handed out to each person to answer. The quiz is an individual endeavor so the staff cannot consult each other.

The answers are posted on the noticeboard in the afternoon. The person who scores the highest mark wins a prize donated by the company.

Time

A new quiz should be prepared each week and handed out on a suitable day when the workload is likely to be lighter

Resource

Photocopier and paper

Prize

Bottle of wine

Benefit

- Gives everyone something to look forward to
- Adds to the enjoyment of work

SOURCE Soula Skliros

The Ultimate Theme Day

The staff of a new department in a bank used this method to introduce themselves to the other departments. They made a big impact, had a lot of fun, and built up the team spirit of their department from the very beginning. One of the managers even did a Scottish dance for all the staff at the end of an evening drinks party.

Purpose

- To bring fun and excitement to the office
- To celebrate a special event, such as an opening of a new location or the introduction of a new department or product

Method

Ask staff for suggestions on a theme for a day and to vote for the one they like best. The person who suggests the winning theme wins a prize.

For example, an International Day might be the winning suggestion. A committee would be needed to coordinate the following:

1. food
2. theme countries for each group of work stations or carousel
3. photography and video of the event
4. presentations at the end of the day.

Each work station or team decorates its area according to the country it represents. Everyone is encouraged to dress according to the country that their team represents. This can bring out amazing creativity.

On the day, the office can organize morning and afternoon teas with an international flavor and invite other departments to attend.

The general manager and company chairperson could be invited to visit the center and select the best dressed person and the best decorated carousel. To finish the day on a high note, everyone could stay back for a drink and to view the video.

Time   One day and lots of lead-up time for preparation to make the day a great success

Resource   Staff willing to spend their own time outside working hours for the preparations; decorations and food

Prize   Bottle of good wine for the best dressed person; dinner for two for each person in the best decorated carousel or work station team

Benefit   • Develops great esprit de corps and pride in the office

SOURCE   Soula Skliros

Trainer's Notes:

Twelve More Theme Day Ideas

Theme days can be very popular events with many offices. Some may want to make them elaborate; others may wish to keep them simple. If you want your theme day to be a success, it is best to check with your staff to see what appeals to them. Theme days are often a great way to celebrate a special day, or can be held just for the fun of it.

Revolting Tie Day

All the men wear their most revolting tie, and everyone votes on the most revolting.

(Lisa Barker)

Shocking Stocking

Staff wear their most outrageous stockings or socks and everyone votes on the most 'shocking'.

(Lisa Barker)

The Snow Theme

Everyone comes to work dressed in snow gear. The staff decorate their area in a winter theme. Prizes are given for the best dressed and best area. Pizza is provided for everyone.

(Mary Kerameas)

Back to Childhood

Everyone brings in a picture of themselves from their school days or at their wedding. These pictures are posted on the wall and the other staff guess who they are and what year they were taken.

Different teams might pick a childhood theme and dress up on the day, for example, as a young basketball team, a baby team, or as fictional characters from story books.

(Sandra Lau)

Hallowe'en

Organize a Hallowe'en cake and have everyone dress in black for the day. But make sure the theme day is something everyone wants—good participation is needed to make it a success.

(Bob Westcott)

Red Day

This is a simple idea that can be used on Valentine's Day or any other day. Everyone dresses in red or in another color that represents something special to the company. Participation is easier than for some of the more complex themes.

(Louise Betts)

Slipper Day

Everyone brings in their favorite or most outrageous slippers and wears them for the day.

(Jeannine Walsh)

St Patrick's Day

Staff wear green and orange to work. The office is decorated in green and orange, and green and orange food is brought in for morning and afternoon tea.

(Bob Westcott)

Race Day

Hold an 'outrageous hat' contest and judge the best creations over a lunch of chicken and champagne.

(Bob Westcott)

Tropical Day

Dress for a day in a tropical paradise, in bright flowery shirts, leis, grass skirts or anything tropical. At the end of the day, play a dictionary game or another game that the group would enjoy.

(Jenni Swistak)

Green Day

Green means go, in other words, 'Go for results'. Everything that people wear, carry and use should be as green as possible but they are not allowed to buy anything new. In a call center, the staff of the inbound section and outbound section could pair up to develop joint green costumes for the day. The best dressed pair wins a prize.

(Sandi Einstein)

Multicultural Day

In an office where there are staff from a variety of cultural backgrounds, choose a day when people dress according to the country of their heritage. They could also bring in food that represents their country and share an international lunch.

(Yvonne Byrne)

The Mad Month

The Mad Month has been a regular feature of St George Direct in Sydney, Australia. The ingenuity and creativity has become legendary. The center decorations become more and more elaborate as the teams work towards the ultimate day, the Mad Day. It perks everyone up, and brushes away those winter blues. This center was voted Top Call Center in Australia in 1995 by the Australian Telemarketing and Call Center Association.

Purpose

- To say goodbye to winter and to welcome in spring
- To create excitement, vitality and enthusiasm in the office
- To have a special month each year that everyone looks forward to

Method

The Mad Month is an extension of the theme day but lasts a whole month.

A theme is chosen by management that will create fun and stimulate ideas. The theme should be suitable for dividing into subthemes. Here are some ideas:

1. **Military might**: The manager becomes the director general, with the office divided into various services—the Army, the Navy, the Air Force, the Nurses Corps and so on.

2. **Zoo theme**: Each group is given the name of a group of animals, such as snakes, cats, monkeys, fish, penguins, and decorates its area in the theme of the animal.

3. **Olympic sports**: Each group picks a sport that most appeals to their group members and decorates its area in this theme.

4. **Holiday theme**: Each group draws a country out of a hat. The groups obtain information and posters for decoration, for example, from embassies and tourist bureaus.

As the month progresses each group decorates its section according to the theme or subtheme. The staff can become more inventive and competitive as the month proceeds.

The month culminates in the Mad Day, when everyone dresses according to their theme. Appropriate food is brought in to be shared and sampled by others in the office.

The children from the company's creche or local day care center could be invited in to see the decorations and people in costumes.

Time

Choose a month near the end of winter

Resource

Staff members' own time, and lots of imagination

Prize

Gift voucher for the best decorated group; gift voucher for the best costume

Benefit

- Contributes to the positive spirit of the office
- Gives people pride in their place of work

SOURCE   Jeannine Walsh

Trainer's Notes:

Slave for the Day

This particular activity has lots of appeal and it can be easily adapted to fit any office, retail or call center situation. What can be more fun than bossing the boss?

Purpose

- Creates fun by working towards an interesting and eventful outcome
- Brings management closer to the staff

Method

Devise a system in which staff can earn 'play money' for accomplishments at work, such as:

1. reaching daily targets
2. handling a high volume of calls
3. displaying a cheerful disposition
4. keeping paperwork up to date
5. being punctual.

Over a three-month period, give people a chance to accumulate their play money earned for the accomplishments. They can work individually or in teams.

At the end of the time period, arrange an auction. The person or team who bids the highest wins the right to have a manager as a slave for the day. To make the auction more fun, have a minimum currency of $50 000. The bidding will be in the millions of dollars.

The manager can be asked to do anything that is work-related for the person or team, such as making morning and afternoon tea, doing the filing or paperwork or handling some of the calls.

Time

Run this over a period of two to three months. Hold the auction after work at the end of the period

Resource

Play money

Reward

Slave for the day

Benefit
- Gives staff another reason to do well
- Helps management to see first-hand what staff do each day

SOURCE Various

Trainer's Notes:

Exercise Day

Sitting all day long can be very tiring. What better way to perk things up than with some exercise? This activity can set the scene for more exercise days in the future. It can also empower staff to energize themselves, by showing them stretches and light exercises they can do near their desks.

Purpose

- To energize the team through exercise
- To encourage 'stretch breaks' and short exercises as an ongoing habit

Method

Select a special day as Exercise Day. On this day, everyone wears gym gear to work. Enlist the help of an occupational nurse or a qualified gym instructor to show the supervisor or team leaders some gentle, easy exercises for people who are sitting down all day.

At regular intervals, team leaders can lead their teams in three to five minutes of exercise. Play upbeat music for exercising, such as 'Let's Get Physical' by Olivia Newton-John.

Provide healthy snacks throughout the day for all the team members, and encourage everyone to drink eight glasses of water on that day.

Time

One day as often as is felt necessary

Resource

Music and fitness posters to set the atmosphere, and healthy snacks

Benefit

- Creates a fun atmosphere
- Gives valuable tips to staff on how to feel more energized during the day

SOURCE Jenni Koch

2

The Fun FACTOR

Appreciation

It's the Little Things That Count

How often have you heard that it is the little things in life that count? Here you will find lots of little things that show staff that management cares about them and appreciates their contributions.

Purpose

- To show your employees that you are thinking about them
- To say 'thank you'

Method

Take every opportunity on a special day to offer a small gift or have a short get-together. Here are a few ideas.

Valentine's Day: Provide everyone with a red rose on their desks.

St Patrick's Day: Get together after work for Irish coffees.

Easter: Have a small basket of Easter eggs on everyone's desk on the day that they break up for Easter.

Launch Day: At the start of a new project, end the first day with a VIP company guest and champagne.

A particularly difficult day: Organize drinks for after work, or send out for pizza to give everyone a 'lift'.

Christmas: Exchange Christmas presents with a $10 limit. Everyone draws a name from a hat and buys a present for that person.

Time

One day for each occasion

Resource

Small budget for gifts, food or beverages

Benefit

- Brightens everyone's day
- Creates a sense of 'family' within the office

SOURCE   Carol York

Staff Appreciation Day

An insurance company combined the staff appreciation day with a theme day. Everyone dressed up like hippies for the day. The managers actually baked the morning tea muffins and biscuits themselves. The key to showing genuine appreciation was in the way they put their baking talents on the line.

Purpose

- To let staff know they are appreciated
- To make staff feel special

Method

Managers designate a Staff Appreciation Day. They can brainstorm all the different ways to show appreciation. They might, for example, serve staff personally with a special morning and afternoon tea, bring in home-baked muffins or biscuits, or give everyone a personalized appreciation certificate.

Incorporate this with a theme day to add extra fun.

Time

Choose one day every six months, when employees need special attention the most

Resource

Morning and afternoon tea

Award

Certificates of appreciation (an example is given on page 27)

Benefit

- Makes staff feel special and appreciated, and encourages them to make customers feel special and appreciated

SOURCE   Rick Barrett

THANK YOU

WELL DONE

In Appreciation

The managers of

_____

would like to show their
appreciation to

_____

by offering *(delete those not applicable)*

cake / a day off / round-the-world cruise /
pizza / salary bonus / company tie /
dinner with a Hollywood star /
burger and french fries / a smile
and a big thank you

With gratitude _____

Surprise Appreciation Day

This is a great method for managers in a panic! The managers know that they need everyone to pull together and go beyond the call of duty, but they just have not had time to think about how to reward the extra effort. They can ask for the results and think of ways to show appreciation as the day progresses.

Purpose

- To demonstrate to employees that the work they do is appreciated
- To show appreciation for some extra effort

Method

The staff members are told that this is not a competition, but they are being asked to do their very best for the day, to boost production or to do their job extremely well for the day.

At the end of the day they will be given a surprise token of appreciation.

Time

Choose one day every six months, when employees need special attention the most

Reward

A gesture that demonstrates appreciation for a job well done

Benefit

- Gives people both a reason and the encouragement to do their best

SOURCE   Sandi Einstein

Trainer's Notes:

The **Appreciation** Award

Eight people from QBE Insurance who were given this award by their company were also nominated and won 'Pride of Workmanship' awards from their local Rotary Club.

Purpose

- To show special appreciation to those who have given extra help after hours

Method

During each quarter in many offices, extra help is needed after hours, for example, to operate the emergency help line over the weekend.

Each month, each quarter and once a year, awards for first, second, and third place can be presented to the people who contribute most hours.

Time

Use monthly, quarterly and annually, or as required

Reward

Cash or gift voucher and a special appreciation plaque. Names can be put on a wall plaque and displayed in the office

Benefit

- Encourages people to volunteer when extra help is needed
- Shows appreciation and recognition for extra effort

SOURCE   Bob Westcott

Trainer's Notes:

The **Thank you** Note

Everyone appreciates the personal touch of a handwritten note, or a personalized certificate that says those powerful words 'Thank You'. This is an easy everyday way to make any staff member feel appreciated.

Purpose

- To give special thanks in a more personal manner for contributions to the job

Method

Keep handy some special letterheads or thank you cards. On a regular basis, write notes of praise or thanks to individual staff members.

Use a computer to make personalized certificates for the staff to say thank you or congratulations on a special accomplishment.

Employees can display these at their work stations.

Time

Use throughout the year

Resource

Thank you notes, computer certificates

Benefit

- Acts as a reminder and a reinforcement of the importance of people's contributions

SOURCE   Soula Skliros; Vicki Jeffery

Trainer's Notes:

The Appreciation Bonus

Let the customer be the judge. This activity will quickly make employees aware of the impression they create with the customer, and will boost sales and customer satisfaction at the same time.

Purpose

- To improve the quality of contacts with regular customers
- To show appreciation to the staff for excellent customer service as rated by their customers

Method

Monthly or quarterly, phone three to five customers at random who deal with the staff member on a regular basis. Ask the customers how they would rank the customer service they receive, on a scale from one to ten. The questions could include:

1. How efficient is our service?
2. How courteously are you treated?
3. Are your expectations met?
4. How would you rate our service overall?

The staff members are paid a customer service appreciation bonus based on how well their customers rank them.

Time

Use monthly or quarterly

Reward

A bonus of up to 50 per cent of salary could be paid, or a smaller bonus according to budget

Benefit

- Leads to dramatic improvements in the quality of customer service
- Stimulates employees to come up with innovative ways to improve customer service

SOURCE   Sandy Perrett

The **Mystery** Envelope

Everyone loves a surprise. This is a method that can be used to reward and reinforce any positive behavior or results. Your local bargain shops are a great place to find the gifts.

Purpose

- To show on the spot reinforcement for positive behavior
- To demonstrate instant appreciation for special contributions
- To help cheer up employees who are feeling discouraged

Method

Organize a box of envelopes of different sizes and colors. In each envelope put a small gift, such as a diary, movie tickets, a lottery ticket, a packet of biscuits or some chocolates. Alternatively, put the name of the gift inside the envelope.

When a show of recognition or appreciation is felt to be appropriate or a member of staff needs cheering up, ask the staff member to select an envelope and receive the gift.

Time

This works best three or four times a year, for one month at a time

Resource

Large container and a range of different envelopes and small gifts

Gift

Try the 'bargain shops' for small gift ideas; also popular are diaries, movie tickets, and lottery tickets

Benefit

- Adds fun and excitement to the day
- Shows employees that they are appreciated
- Helps employees overcome a discouraging moment

SOURCE Bill St James

Customer Bouquets

Nothing beats a personal testimonial from a satisfied customer. This is a great way to make the most of that honor for the staff member who is being praised.

Purpose

- To let everyone know when someone has been thanked or praised by a customer

Method

A customer bouquet is a letter to the company praising one of the staff members. Display these letters on a noticeboard in the staff room (a frame is provided on page 35) and send letters of congratulations through e-mail for all to see.

Sometimes pleased customers may not write a letter but may mention their appreciation to a supervisor or team leader. When this happens, the supervisor should ensure that this praise is passed on to the staff member and written up, so that everyone in the organization is aware of it.

These customer bouquets can also be put in the employees' files. When the end of year awards are decided, the letters could be used as one of the bases for awards.

Time

Keep this as a regular feature

Resource

A prominent noticeboard and eye-catching 'frames' (see page 35)

Benefit

- Reinforces the type of behavior that is to be encouraged

SOURCE   Sandra Lau

A Message from a Grateful Customer

The Most Motivated
and the Whinger's Award

The staff at this cosmetics company put their heads together and created their own weekly award. It has been a great hit. Everyone can nominate who they appreciate and poke some fun at something they did not appreciate. It is light-hearted and staff look forward to Friday afternoons when winners are announced.

Purpose

- To help to maintain the positive atmosphere of the office
- To give everyone a vehicle through which to praise the efforts of other people on the team, and to handle with humor a situation when some staff complain too much

Method

At the end of the week, everyone nominates someone for the Most Motivated. They write down the name of the person and what the person did.

Names may also be submitted for the Whinger's Award. Encourage humor and light-hearted fun. The nomination should include the name of the person and their 'whinge'.

When all the nominations are in, read them out to everyone. (If any of the Whinger's Award nominations are too sensitive or inappropriate, simply do not read them.) The team leader is the judge and selects the winners.

Time

Great fun when held weekly

Resource

Nomination forms (see the examples); small prize of $5 or $10 value

Benefit

- Allows people to voice their appreciation of each other
- Gives a chance to let off steam
- Encourages a positive atmosphere

SOURCE   Jane Burgess

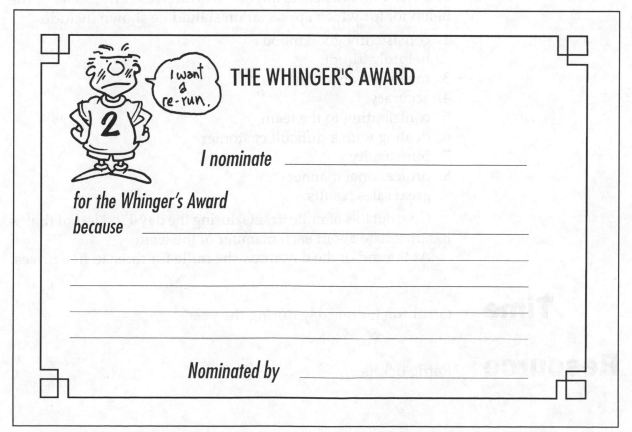

THE MOST MOTIVATED AWARD

I nominate _____

for the Most Motivated Award
because _____
_____
_____
_____
_____

Nominated by _____

THE WHINGER'S AWARD

I want a re-run.

I nominate _____

for the Whinger's Award
because _____
_____
_____
_____

Nominated by _____

The Appreciation **Raffle**

The team leaders of this bank were looking for an easy, cost-effective way to show appreciation, encourage positive behavior and have a bit of fun. The appreciation raffle was a result of their brainstorming. This can work in almost any office, retail outlet or call center environment.

Purpose

• To provide another way of saying 'thank you'
• To highlight a way of reinforcing positive behavior in the office

Method

Choose a day on which to hold a surprise appreciation raffle. On that day, hand out raffle tickets for anything the staff do that is impressive or deserves appreciation. Staff should bring to attention on that day anything for which they feel they have not been appreciated. For doing this, they also receive a raffle ticket.

Give raffle tickets to everyone who comes to work on time, and two raffle tickets to anyone who arrives early. Some of the behavior for which appreciation should be shown includes:

1. consistently good mood
2. helpful attitude
3. meeting a deadline
4. accuracy
5. contributing to the team
6. dealing with a difficult customer
7. punctuality
8. professional manner
9. great sales results.

Give out lots of raffle tickets during the day. Find lots of things to appreciate about each member of the team.

At the end of the day, draw the raffle for three to five prizes.

Time

Great fun for one day during the year

Resource

Raffle tickets

Prize

Prizes under the value of $10 that would appeal to team members

Benefit

- Helps the team leader focus on the positive instead of negative actions of the staff
- Gives the team leader a way of saying 'I appreciate you'
- Makes employees feel special

SOURCE

Nina Pennisi; Lavina Siumaka; Kylie Black; Gae Baumann

Trainer's Notes:

The **Treasure Chest**

This credit union had undergone a lot of change. The managers felt that the staff needed to feel better about themselves and to appreciate their own accomplishments more. The Treasure Chest was a way for them to make this happen.

Purpose

- To encourage self-appreciation
- To focus on the positive actions and results of each day
- To encourage positive behavior

Method

Provide a box and a pad of paper for each of the employees in your office. Ask them to write down at the end of the day something they did that they are really pleased about or proud of. Do this for two weeks, writing down different accomplishments of which they are proud. At the end of two weeks, sit down with each employee to go through the 'treasure chest' of points they have written down.

Time

Do this every two weeks

Resource

Cardboard or plastic box, pads of paper

Benefit

- Makes the manager aware of what people are proud of
- Gives the staff members a chance to praise themselves
- Gives managers a better insight into the people they manage

SOURCE   Kaye Wetzler

Trainer's Notes:

3

The **Fun** FACTOR

Competition

The New Sales Week

The Monday to Friday sales week time frame has its limitations. This manager noticed that the staff were slow to get started on Mondays, Tuesdays and even Wednesdays. Thursdays and Fridays were always great days, as everyone put in the extra effort to achieve budget. By changing the working week as described below, every day became more productive.

Purpose

• To boost sales or production on normally slow days

Method

When a sales week runs from Monday to Friday, production is often slow on Mondays and sales results are often excellent on Fridays as everyone strives to meet their weekly targets.

Try changing the sales week, for example, starting on Wednesday and ending on Tuesday. When the sales people arrive at work on Monday, they will experience a sense of urgency—and Friday will still be a great sales results day.

Paying people commission on a weekly basis is also very motivating. End the sales week on Tuesday and pay commissions on Friday.

Early in the sales cycle, create incentives based on the number of sales instead of the dollar value of sales. This encourages activity. Near the end of the sales week, use incentives that reward the dollar amount. This gives extra encouragement to reach weekly targets.

Pay a bonus on the number of sales rather than on the amount of the sales. The sales person who has made a big sale and may have mentally 'given up' for the rest of the week will be encouraged to keep working. However, commission should still be paid on the total dollar value of the sales.

Time

Arrange this system on a weekly basis

Benefit

• Increases production on days that are normally slow
• Adds new interest and excitement to the sales week

SOURCE   Simon Petersen

The **Casino** Challenge

It is always fun to tie in a competition with an event that is taking place in your city. For example, the first casino was opening in this city so the manager used this event and designed a competition around it. Of course this is also a fun competition that could be used at any time.

Purpose

- To focus on selling a particular product through a team competition
- To use a forthcoming event to stimulate interest and direct employees' attention to a particular sales area
- To draw a range of people into teams and use each other's strengths to work towards a common goal, thus improving morale in the office

Method

Organize teams in the office, taking into account the different selling strengths of the employees so that the teams are evenly matched.

Nominate a particular product on which the competition will be focused. Set an enquiry conversion or sales goal for each team to achieve, for each day or week during the period of the competition.

Each time a team achieves its conversion or sales goal for the product, it receives casino chips or tokens.

At the end of the competition, the teams can trade in their chips for a group prize.

Time

Hold over a period of one to two months, or during a period of build-up to an important or exciting event

Prizes

Gift vouchers or dinner for two

Resource

Casino chips or tokens; a visual display could be devised to show the ongoing achievements of each team, using the casino theme and the promise of a 'jackpot' for the winners

Benefit

- Helps to increase production or sale of a specific product or service
- Creates an atmosphere in which team members encourage and assist each other

SOURCE   Soula Skliros

Trainer's Notes:

The **Phone-Out** Award

As soon as this team award was announced, the volume of outbound calls went up, and they stayed up. Sales increased, too.

Purpose

- To increase the number of outbound calls that the telephone sales people complete in a week

Method

Divide the telephone sales people into teams (this will not be necessary if they are already working in teams). Set as the expected standard a minimum number of outbound calls you expect to be made by each person every week. The team that makes the most outbound calls by the end of the week wins the weekly bonus.

Time

Use this on a weekly basis

Award

A set weekly bonus

Benefit

- Helps to overcome 'call reluctance'
- Increases the number of outbound calls through positive peer pressure
- Improves productivity generally

SOURCE   Lisa Barker

The **Cross-Selling** Challenge

This manager had been struggling with ways to get all the sales staff (and not just the top sales people) to offer and sell other related products. After many different attempts, she found this method achieved the results she was looking for.

Purpose

- To increase production by improving everyone's cross-selling results

Method

The sales staff are asked to improve their results and make more bonuses by selling additional products or services. They each select one of five targets that they feel they can realistically achieve for the month. It must be a target that they are prepared to meet. For each target, a dollar value bonus will be assigned.

Each month, the sales staff can select a new target as they become more confident.

Time

Continuous during each sales cycle

Bonus

A dollar bonus that increases for each increased target level

Benefit

- Helps people to improve their sales results through a gradual process
- Increases confidence among the sales staff as they achieve success and are rewarded for it
- Indicates who might need additional help or training

SOURCE Soula Skliros

Trainer's Notes:

Let's **Race**

Sometimes the hardest part of selling is just starting. This method is used very successfully by the manager of a stationery company to get the ball rolling and the sales coming after the weekend break.

Purpose

- To kick-start sales activity or pick up the pace when it needs a boost.
- To add motivation to a Monday morning

Method

Announce to all the sales staff that there will be a sales race for the next three hours. Ask them to have everything organized on their desks that they will need while selling. Set up a sales board in an accessible place.

Ring the start bell and the sales race begins. The first, second, third, fourth and fifth people to achieve a confirmed sale with a complete, written-up order win a bonus.

To claim a bonus, the staff member must race to the sales board to write up the sale. Often, two people will make a sale at the same time. The person who reaches the sales board first wins.

For a variation on the Let's Race game, the sale of a certain amount could be specified, or the sale of a particular product.

Time

Half a day at a time could be spent on this, at slower periods in the week

Resource

Sales board to write up the sales

Bonus

Appropriate cash prizes, for example, first place—$50; second place—$40; third place—$30; fourth place—$20; fifth place—$10

Benefit

- Gives everyone a 'kick-start'
- Overcomes 'call reluctance'
- Appeals to the competitive spirit of the sales staff

SOURCE Simon Petersen

New Business Competition

Sometimes staff need a competition to help them focus on the area the management is targeting. This New Business Competition gives the staff the incentive they need to bring in new customers.

Purpose

- To focus on opening new accounts

Method

Announce to the sales staff that a competition will be held, aimed at bringing in new business. Give them several ways to win, for example:

1. Every time they gain a new account and an initial order, they are given a raffle ticket for a chance to win a prize.
2. When they reach a personal target that has been set for them, they are given a bonus.
3. The sales person who opens the most new accounts wins a prize.
4. The sales person who brings in the most business from new customers wins a prize.

Time

Hold the competition once every three months

Resource

Chart to track progress; raffle tickets

Prize

Portable CD players, dinner for two, gift vouchers

Benefit

- Improves the skills needed to open new accounts
- Increases business

SOURCE   Mary Kerameas

Auction Fun

The staff of a newspaper company loved this day. It has been repeated at different times in different departments and always with great results. Staff loved the fun and anticipation created in the day. Everyone loved the results achieved.

Purpose

- To boost sales production in a cross-section of areas
- To create fun and lift morale for the day
- To show people what they are capable of accomplishing

Method

1. Determine some specific areas that are to be encouraged and rewarded for the period of the game, for example:
   - total revenue generated
   - a type of product
   - a range of products
   - amount of individual sales
   - number of sales.

   Assign a points value to each of these areas.
2. At the end of the day or week, tally each person's points and exchange the points for Monopoly money or tokens that can be spent at the auction. (Make your own play money, similar to that shown on page 51.)
3. Select an auctioneer—someone who is fun and a bit crazy. Provide snacks and drinks to create a party atmosphere.
4. Provide a range of prizes of various value. Either wrap them so that no one knows what is inside the packages or let everyone see them.
5. The auctioneer starts the bidding and the staff bid for the prizes. Allow them to pool their Monopoly money if they wish.

Time

Hold over one day, one week or one month, as required

Resource

Monopoly or play money or tokens

Prize

A whole range of both crazy and useful prizes that would appeal to your group

Benefit

- Builds staff morale
- Creates a team spirit
- Increases sales

SOURCE Gabby Hockey

The 100 Club

This long-term competition is one everyone can participate in and work towards. Every year the company has a new travel destination to create excitement and anticipation.

The monthly Achievers' Breakfast keeps everyone on track towards the major goal.

Purpose

- To give everyone an extra motivation for reaching 100 per cent of the budget
- To reward and recognize the achievement

Method

The 100 Club can begin each February and continue for the next seven months. Each person is given a monthly budget based on experience, territory, and the time of year. It is important for the sales person to understand why their budget has been set for them and to believe that it is achievable.

Every month, those who achieve 100 per cent of their budget are invited to attend the Achievers' Breakfast.

At the end of the seventh month, every sales person who has achieved an average of 100 per cent of budget wins a five-day trip for two to a destination chosen for that year.

Time

Hold monthly for seven months

Award

Plaques; Achievers' Breakfast; five-day trip for two

Benefit

- Focuses on both long-term and short-term goals
- Gives recognition on a monthly basis

SOURCE   Mary Kerameas

Valentine's Day Hearts

The visual aspect of this competition creates lots of interest and fun. The staff at this newspaper company love the fact that everyone can win many times over. They also become aware of what other people are doing to achieve sales, and use these techniques too. It is fun for everyone, and creates an immediate learning experience.

Purpose

- To encourage and reward the practice of cross-selling, leading up to a special day, such as Valentine's Day

Method

A large red heart is made from paper or cardboard and stuck on the wall for all to see. Small hearts are stuck randomly around the big heart. On the back of each small heart, the value of a prize is written—for example, $1, $5 or $10.

Each time one of the sales people cross-sells a particular item, that person chooses a heart from the wall as a reward.

This activity can be adapted for St Patrick's Day, May Day, Hallowe'en, Thanksgiving or any other day of celebration.

Time

Two weeks leading up to the special day

Resource

Large sheets of red paper or cardboard to make the hearts; other decorative material

Prize

Certificate indicating $1, $5 or $10 value, to be paid as part of the employee's monthly bonus

Benefit

- Provides a fun way to celebrate a special day
- Reinforces the skills needed to cross-sell
- Improves sales for the period

SOURCE   Sandra Lau

Lucky Dip

How outrageous do you want your lucky dips to be?! The staff of this stationery company appreciated the ridiculous and irreverent nature of their lucky dip prizes.

Purpose

• To boost energy on a Monday morning
• To act as a kick-start to sales activity

Method

Put together a big box of gift-wrapped presents. The presents should be as crazy and silly as possible. Find them in joke shops, bargain shops or toy stores. Include a few useful gifts.

Every Monday morning until midday, the members of the sales team can pick a lucky dip for each sale that they make, until all the lucky dips are gone.

Time

One half day, or until the lucky dips have all been claimed

Resource

Big box; lucky dip gifts; wrapping paper

Gift

Anything outrageous that will cause laughter, but keep the value under $3

Benefit

• Injects laughter into a Monday morning
• Boosts sales in a period that is usually slow

SOURCE   Simon Petersen

Trainer's Notes:

The Project Raffle

It can be boring if the best sales person always wins. This competition gives everyone lots of chances to win. Every time any member of the sales staff makes a sale, they get a chance to win the big prize.

Purpose

- To add extra excitement to a special sales campaign
- To offer an extra benefit to the sales person for achieving a sale

Method

When each different telephone sales or other sales project begins, hold a raffle associated with it. Every time the sales person makes a sale, they also get a raffle ticket. At the end of each shift they collect their raffle tickets. When the project is finished, all the tickets go into the draw for a major prize.

Time

Keep this going for the duration of the project

Resource

Raffle tickets and a visual display of the prize

Prize

Dinner for two, or a weekend away for two

Benefit

- Adds fun and excitement to the project
- Creates a game of chance where anyone can win, regardless of experience

SOURCE   Bill St James

Trainer's Notes:

The Friday Night CD Draw

Having staffing problems on those unpopular shifts? Hold out a carrot that will motivate staff to show up. Once this organization started the CD raffle, absenteeism ceased to be a problem.

Purpose

- To encourage staff to work an unpopular shift

Method

It can sometimes be difficult to achieve full staffing of casual and permanent employees for the unpopular Friday or Saturday night shift. Absenteeism is discouraged if everyone at work on the Friday evening shift goes into the draw for a CD voucher.

Time

Make this a regular Friday or Saturday night event

Prize

CD voucher

Benefit

- Improves attendance dramatically on unpopular nights
- Boosts production on a shift that is no longer affected by absenteeism

SOURCE   Bill St James

Key Performance Indicators

This motivation method recognizes that staff performance is based on many aspects of their contributions. This international company uses the Key Performance Indicators as a way to determine a large percentage of the annual salary of their sales team.

Purpose

- To help sales people focus on the key performance areas of their jobs
- To give sales people a structure through which to increase their annual salary by 50 per cent

Method

Each sales person is given a monthly goal based on experience, territory and the time of year. This goal covers four key areas:
1. monthly gross profit
2. targeted mix of products
3. size of the order and introduction of new products
4. retention of the top fifty customers.

A bonus up to 50 per cent of annual salary can be earned by the sales person based on their performance in these four areas. The key performance indicators are tracked monthly so the sales person knows exactly how they are doing. The bonus is paid quarterly.

Time

Annually: tracked monthly, and paid quarterly

Bonus

Up to 50 per cent of annual salary

Benefit

- Helps people focus on a wider range of selling opportunities
- Gives staff a clear indication of what management expects
- Allows people to see their efforts as a contribution towards the company's goals and vision

SOURCE   Mary Kerameas

The Sliding Hourly Rate

For many, commission is often a scary or unobtainable goal. Break it down into an hourly figure and it soon seems to be more obtainable. This organization has found that the staff value their own time more when they are paid according to a sliding hourly scale.

Purpose

- To pay people according to their average hourly production

Method

Each sales person is paid the same basic hourly rate. In order to increase this rate, the sales person must increase the average sales per hour. For example, if the basic hourly rate is $11 per hour, this rate can fluctuate upwards to, say, $13 or $17 or even $55 per hour, depending on the person's average hourly sales rate.

At the end of each day, then at the end of the week, the sales people are given their average hourly sales figures and pay is calculated accordingly. They are paid at the end of each week whichever is higher—the weekly average or by taking each day separately.

Time

Use on a weekly basis

Resource

A clear 'tracking system' so that everyone knows exactly where they stand

Reward

Increased earnings based on individual effort

Benefit

- Helps sales people to focus on the immediacy of their jobs— each hour is important

SOURCE   Bill St James

Double Dare

This competition is a perfect example of how you can combine two different competitions to make the challenge more intriguing for the staff.

Purpose

- To boost production for the day or week
- To add some excitement and reward for effort

Method

Set a target for each sales person for the morning. Those sales people who meet their morning sales targets then receive double commission for all sales in the afternoon.

Combine this with a lucky dip. Make up packages that contain three small gifts instead of only one, to add to the interest and excitement of receiving a lucky dip. For example, one lucky dip prize could be a box of chocolates, movie tickets and a hair brush.

The sales person with the most sales each hour picks from the box of lucky dips. This will keep up the interest of those who are not on double commission for the afternoon.

Time

One day, or five days for one week

Resource

Gifts for the lucky dip

Benefit

- Adds fun to the day
- Provides a real sales and morale booster

SOURCE   Bill Avery

Trainer's Notes:

The Horse Race

The success of any competition depends on the enthusiasm that the manager can demonstrate. If you use the horse race, become the race steward, and bring in a pair of binoculars to view the results several times during the day. This should cause a ripple of laughter.

Purpose

- To display everyone's production rate visually, in a fun and interesting way
- To stimulate sales through a 'race' contest

Method

Cut the shapes of horses out of cardboard and allocate one to each sales person, with their names and the names of the horses on them. The sales people can pick names for their horses that indicate something about their own personalities.

On a wall or a glass partition in the office, pin up all the horses at the 'starting gate'. As the month progresses, move the horses as the sales people generate sales or leads. Some of the less experienced sales people may be given a head start.

The horse that reaches the winning post first wins the race and that sales person wins a gift voucher.

Time

Hold the race over a one-month period

Resource

Cardboard to cut out horses and decorations for the 'track' on the wall

Prize

Gift voucher

Benefit

- Improves sales
- Increases people's awareness of their own production rate in relation to others

SOURCE   Alex Harper

Name _____

The Christmas Tree Competition

When the Christmas tree arrives, everyone gets into the spirit!
What is a Christmas tree without presents underneath it? Who
will unwrap the presents? The winners of this competition.

Purpose

- To focus on cross-selling or up-selling a specific product or
service

Method

Under the office Christmas tree, put a whole range of presents.
    Each time a sales person cross-sells or up-sells a certain
product or service, that person receives a raffle ticket. The prizes
in the raffle are the gifts under the Christmas tree.
    One week before Christmas, draw the raffle and organize a
prize for the team that has the most tickets.

Time

Five weeks before Christmas up to the week prior to Christmas

Resource

Christmas tree, raffle tickets, prizes

Gifts

Christmas cakes, puddings, chocolates, champagne, Christmas
decorations or anything with a Christmas theme

Benefit

- Celebrates the Christmas season in a fun way
- Keeps up the sales momentum before Christmas
- Helps develop the habit of cross-selling

SOURCE   Sandra Lau

Pin the Tail for a **Sale**

This is a back-to-childhood game. It will conjure up memories of the fun of children's birthday parties. A competition that gives people an excuse to act like children is always fun.

Purpose

- To offer a daily reward for reaching the sales target
- To give the sales people an extra reason to achieve the daily target

Method

Purchase a 'Pin the tail on the donkey' game from a toy store or make one. Place the donkey prominently on a wall.

Each person who achieves the sales target for the day wins a donkey's tail. The person who achieves the target first and the person who sells the most earn an extra 'tail' to pin on the donkey.

At the end of the day, blindfold the people who have won 'tails' and play 'Pin the tail on the donkey'. The person who sticks a tail closest to the correct position on the donkey wins the daily prize.

Time

One day, or every day for one week

Resource

'Pin the tail on the donkey' game, blindfold

Prize

CD voucher, cash prize, bottle of wine (vary the prizes for each day)

Benefit

- Helps to boost daily production
- Gives an opportunity for friendly competition
- Creates fun and boosts morale

SOURCE   Carolyn Greenwich

63

The Mystery Squares

This particular competition created so much interest within this computer company that the sales results of the targeted product rose significantly over the same period of the previous year. The cost of the contest proved to be a great investment.

Purpose

- To encourage sales people who sell a range of products to focus on increasing sales of a specific product or service of a nominated dollar value

Method

This is a sales game that revolves around mystery squares. Use a white board or make a large square from cardboard. Divide the board into about 50 mystery squares, numbering each square. The number on each square will correspond to a mystery prize. The value of the prizes can vary dramatically and one could be of far greater value than the rest, such as $1000.

Every time sales people sell the specified products or services of a certain dollar value, they can put their name on a square and claim the mystery prize at the end of the game.

None of the mystery prizes are revealed until all the squares are claimed or the time allowed for the game is up. Lots of excitement is created as everyone tries to guess exactly where the big prize is.

At the end of the time period, hold an upbeat sales meeting with dinner or drinks to reveal the prizes that everyone has won.

Time

Hold over a one to two month period

Resource

White board and magnetic stickers, or large colored cardboard

Prize

T-shirts, sweat shirts, travel games, dinner vouchers, candy, wine, baseball hats, CDs, a cash prize or voucher worth $1000, three cash prizes or vouchers worth $200

Benefit

- Increases the production of the team
- Creates a sense of fun, anticipation and excitement
- Motivates team members to learn and use new sales skills
- Creates the habit of selling a particular product or service

SOURCE Mike Kleviansky

Trainer's Notes:

The **Travel** Gift Voucher Bonus

This competition is designed to satisfy some of people's travel lust. What better way to enjoy a holiday than to have won all or part of it in a sales competition?

Purpose

- To reward and recognize the top achiever in your team

Method

This bonus is based on a points system. Points are awarded for a variety of accomplishments, such as:

1. number of outbound calls
2. entries into the database
3. number of sales in a variety of areas
4. retention of accounts
5. generation of a sales lead.

The participants in the competition are involved in setting the base level of points needed to qualify for the bonus. If no one reaches this base level, there is no reward. The manager helps to set the target level by asking the question: 'What do you regard as excellent?' This prevents the participants from setting the qualifying target too low.

It is important to have a clear tracking system. Points should be counted every month.

Time

Hold over a period of four months

Resource

Instruction sheet on the rules and points system of the game and a clear tracking system on which to record results once a month

Prize

A travel gift voucher

Benefit

- Gives clear directions on the areas of achievement that are considered important
- Gives sales people a way of comparing their results with those of their peers

SOURCE   Lisa Barker

The **Budget** Buster Dinner

This is a fun way to turn a regular get-together into an incentive to improve performance or meet budget.

Purpose

• To encourage staff to work towards their monthly budgets

Method

Each sales person is given a monthly budget based on experience, client base and time of year. The budget is carefully explained so that they see their targets as achievable.

At the end of the month, everyone gets together for dinner. If they have all achieved their budgets, management pays for dinner. If they have not, then everyone pays for their own meal.

At the dinner, a special prize is given to those who have exceeded their budgets.

Time

Hold on a monthly basis

Resource

Visual display of progress of each sales person

Prize

Management pays for dinner when everyone meets budget; dinner for two/a weekend away for those who exceed budget

Benefit

• Makes the sales people encourage each other to achieve budget
• Rewards group effort

SOURCE   Vasilis Karbouris

It's fun when the boss is paying

Frequent Seller Club

This is a twist on the frequent flyer clubs. The more the sales people sell, the more points they earn to spend on a selection of useful or fun gift items.

Purpose

- To encourage sales people through an individual incentive scheme to focus either on sales of one product or on overall production on a regular basis

Method

Introduce the Frequent Seller Club to the sales team. The club can either have specific starting and finishing dates or can be ongoing.

For each product or service sold or for each dollar amount sold, the sales people receive points. The aim is to accumulate as many points as they can. At the end or at various intervals, they can redeem their points from a selection of prizes. Encourage the sales people to set a goal by targeting the prize that they want to win.

There could be six different value levels of prizes with a range of prizes in each level that appeal to the tastes of the sales staff. Ask for suggestions before starting the Frequent Seller Club. Display the pictures of prizes visually on a wall. Hold a presentation of the prizes for everyone to attend.

Time

Continuously or over a six month period

Resource

Display of prizes

Prize

Assorted prizes, from a value of $50 up to the sixth level of prizes worth $500

Benefit

- Gives the sales staff something to anticipate and work towards
- Rewards people for reaching a long-term goal

SOURCE Various

Set Your Next Quarter's Salary

For this insurance company the act of spreading commission over a three-month period proved very beneficial to all concerned. They also found that, even if staff were away sick or on holidays during the period, they always managed to meet budget.

Purpose

- To enable the sales staff to increase their salary level for each quarter

Method

Sales staff are told that their salary is based on an individual benchmark budget. If they meet and exceed their budget by 20 per cent or 50 per cent over a three-month period, their salary for the next three months is increased by the performance bonus.

No allowance is made for time off due to sickness or holidays. The performance bonus is paid fortnightly with the salary during the next quarter.

Time

Hold this quarterly

Reward

Performance bonus paid fortnightly over the following quarter

Benefit

- Gives people two performance goals on which to focus
- Spreads out the reward by paying the bonus fortnightly
- Motivates the sales staff who are away due to sickness or holidays to meet their targets regardless

SOURCE Judy Purdon

On the Spot Incentive

Solve the wonderful problem of what to do when someone does something beyond expectations! The best acknowledgment is immediate acknowledgment.

Purpose

- To give an incentive for extra effort

Method

Put in place an incentive that can be given immediately to encourage and reward certain achievements. The award should be for a non-sales achievement, for example:
1. for coming up with a great idea
2. for receiving a letter of praise from a customer
3. for displaying excellent team work
4. for providing excellent customer service.

Time

Give to a staff member whenever it is deserved

Award

$50 gift voucher; certificate (example on page 71)

Benefit

- Rewards staff member for displaying a good attitude
- Encourages excellent customer service in the sales environment

SOURCE   Lisa Barker

Trainer's Notes:

Extra Effort
Award

This is to certify that

_____

has been awarded a
special prize of _____

_____

for

_____

Logo Competition

The word game enthusiasts in the office will have fun with this competition. It is an easy game to set up and will help boost production any day or for a month of the year.

Purpose

- To race to sell a particular number or range of products or services

Method

Pick a word that represents something within the company, preferably a word that has between three and five letters.

The first sales person or team to 'spell' the word wins a prize in the competition. Specify a starting time for the contest. To obtain a letter in the word, they need to achieve a specific goal. For example if the word is 'logo', to spell the word they would need to achieve the following:

L = Make twenty sales.
O = Make a mix of product sales.
G = Make five sales of a certain size.
O = Complete 100 outbound calls.

Time

Competition could last anywhere from a day to three months

Resource

Scoring sheet and a tracking system that everyone can see

Prize

Anything under $15

Benefit

- Helps sales people to focus on all the different results they need to achieve
- Creates a sense of fun for sales people who like word games

SOURCE   Sandra Lau

Balloon Busters

There is nothing like a balloon bursting to get energy going in the office! This very visual month-long competition keeps up interest and brings in results for the bank in which it is used.

Purpose

- To create a sense of fun and excitement in selling
- To provide an incentive to sell more

Method

Have a huge banner hanging on the wall above a noticeboard that says 'Balloon Busters'. Decorate the whole department with balloons. Inside each balloon put a number that corresponds to a small prize.

Every time a sales person sells a product or service of a certain value, they can burst either one or two balloons and receive the specified prize.

The name of the sales person who bursts the most balloons for the day is posted on the Balloon Busters noticeboard. Each day during the month, new names are added to the board.

Each week, a prize of more value can be added to the balloons, for example, $30. At the end of the competition the sales person who has sold the most is awarded a special prize as Balloon Buster of the month.

Time

Hold for one month per year

Resource

Balloons, banner and noticeboard

Prize

Small prizes, such as candy bars or vouchers; special prize, such as a gift voucher for $50 or $100

Benefit

- Adds excitement and fun to the day each time a balloon is burst
- Motivates the sales people to sell more

SOURCE   Soula Skliros

Beat the Boss

This activity offers a quick way to combine training by example with a competition to stimulate sales results. It gives everyone involved a new challenge and a fun reason to succeed.

Purpose

- To demonstrate to the sales staff the ability of the 'boss' to sell
- To lead by example
- To give sales staff the incentive to 'beat the boss'

Method

Set aside a day when the supervisor or 'boss' can sell all day. In a call center environment this works well for a specific inbound or outbound campaign that generates an immediate result or sale. In a retail outlet choose a day that is usually busy.

Nominate a specific starting and finishing time and measure each person's production or sales in that time, including those of the 'boss'. All the people who beat the boss's production or the sales staff member who comes closest share in a cash reward.

Time

Great fun once a year

Prize

$100 cash divided among the winners

Benefit

- Gives people an extra boost to achieve
- Allows sales staff to learn by watching and listening to the 'boss' in action
- Helps the boss to appreciate and understand the challenges that sales staff members face every day

SOURCE   Carolyn Greenwich

Pick a Chick

One of the most popular segments of a TV program that has been running in Australia for 25 years (called *Hey Hey It's Saturday*) is 'Pluck a Duck'. This program is the inspiration for Pick a Chick. It is a fun visual game that also involves a local school. The sales people at this company love the game and keep the children's pictures at their work stations long after the game is finished.

Purpose

- To boost individual sales performance
- To involve both sales and non-sales people in boosting sales production

Method

Provide a local primary school with all the drawing and decorative materials that they need to make about thirty pictures of chickens. A small donation could be made to the school art department for their efforts.

Display the pictures on a wall in the office. On the back of each picture, write a number that corresponds to a prize. The list of prizes should be kept under lock and key. Every time a sales person reaches a certain number of sales, that person is able to 'Pick a Chick' and win the corresponding prize.

When the sales team reaches the group target for the week, the non-sales staff put all their names in a hat. The person whose name is drawn also gets to 'Pick a Chick'.

Time

Continuously for the length of a project or until all the chickens have been 'picked'

Resource

Art material for the local primary school

Prize

Facials, hair appointments, dinners, weekends away, gift vouchers

Benefit

- Involves the whole office in the reward scheme
- Provides community involvement
- Creates fun and increases sales

SOURCE   Ian Low

Marshmallow Madness

This game is similar to the guessing game, 'Guess how many beans are in the jar'. It gives everyone a chance to win if they reach their target, and it provides a fun excuse for a get-together at the end of the week for hot chocolate and marshmallows!

Purpose

• To reward sales people for reaching or exceeding their target

Method

Fill a huge jar full of marshmallows. Each sales person who reaches a target for the week can guess how many marshmallows are in the jar. At the end of the week, the number of marshmallows in the jar is revealed. The five people who came closest or guessed the exact number win. Five different prizes could be provided. The person who came closest picks a prize first, and the person who came fifth picks last.

Provide everyone in the office with hot chocolate in which to enjoy the marshmallows.

Time

This can become a weekly event

Resource

Marshmallows and a large jar (change the size of the jar each week or use other types of candy to add variety)

Prize

Movie tickets, wine, chocolates, dinner

Benefit

• Provides an inexpensive but fun way to give rewards
• Gives everyone a chance to win

SOURCE   Graeme Baker

Christmas Mural

Some sales staff either wind down as Christmas approaches, or get so busy that they miss opportunities to cross-sell other products. This game will solve either of these possibilities by helping staff to become focused on products to promote and targets to meet. It is very visual, and adds to the Christmas fun.

Purpose

- To provide a fun pre-Christmas activity
- To boost sales during a slower time

Method

Organize the staff to make a huge Christmas mural, or ask a local primary school to make one for the office. The mural should have twenty-four doors on it. Under each of the doors will be the name of a prize, or a number that corresponds to a secret prize.

Twenty-four days before Christmas, place the Christmas mural on the wall. Each day, decide on a different target, for example, a specific product, a group of products, or a dollar amount of sales. Each day, the person who reaches the target first can choose a door and win the prize for the day.

Time

Twenty-four days in the run-up to Christmas

Resource

Mural materials

Prize

A selection of prizes of different value (suppliers of the products that the team is selling could provide the prize for the day on which their product is targeted)

Benefit

- Allows people of different abilities and sales strengths to win
- Increases sales

SOURCE   Susan Williams

Daily Darts

A quick, fun and easy game that can be adapted to almost any sales situation. Any darts experts should be disadvantaged so that everyone is on a similar level of ability.

Purpose

- To create a daily focus on production
- To help overcome sales reluctance

Method

Buy a dartboard from a sports shop. Place it permanently on the wall in a safe corner of the staff room, so that everyone can practise their skills during breaks.

Each day, the sales staff earn one chance at the dartboard for every sale they make. At the end of the day, the sales staff gather to throw their darts. The person with the highest score wins a prize.

Another version of this game is called 'Survival'. It can be played once or twice a week to make the darts game more interesting. Each sales staff member draws three numbers before playing darts. If they hit these numbers, they automatically disqualify themselves.

Before you start the game, arrange for everyone to play darts and judge how good they are. The really good players can be made to play with their left hand.

Time

Hold daily for one to two weeks

Resource

Dartboard, darts

Prize

Prizes under the value of $20 that would appeal to the sales staff

Benefit

- Gives the sales staff another reason to sell
- Gives everyone a chance to win
- Provides an after-work activity to look forward to

SOURCE   Luke Carey; Matthew Carney

Bingo Breakthrough

This popular game will cause lots of excitement in the office. Ask suppliers to become involved by contributing prizes for the game.

Purpose

- To improve the sales of a wide range of products and services
- To improve cross-selling and up-selling skills

Method

Nominate twenty-four different sales targets for the sales people to accomplish over a period of a month. These may range from particular dollar amounts or a quantity of items in the product range to the opening up of a given number of new accounts.

On a bingo card provided for each sales person, write a sales target clearly in each box. Some targets may appear more than once. Make the middle box a 'free' box.

Each sales person has a chance to win bingo by crossing a box when the particular target has been met.

Whenever a sales person completes a line of crosses horizontally, vertically, diagonally or has crosses on the four corners, that person rings a bell and wins a prize or a bonus.

Time

Hold over a one-month period

Resource

Personalized bingo cards; a bell

Prize/Bonus

Ask suppliers to contribute to a range of prizes or arrange a bonus that accelerates in value as each sales person gets more 'bingos'

Benefit

- Promotes sales of a wide range of products
- Builds staff morale as everyone has an equal chance to win
- Moves products that management wants to move

SOURCE Susan Williams

Hot Shot

The movie *Hot Shots* is the inspiration for this game. A version of it was first used as a branch office competition. It can also be used as an individual competition, as shown below.

Purpose
- To provide a month of fun activities and competition around the themes 'Hot' and 'Hot Shot'
- To increase sales results
- To help individuals boost their performance

Method

In the Hot Shot competition, every week for a month there are winners in the categories below. The awards can be for the individual, the team or both.
1. The Hot Shot: Best Weekly Production
2. The Hottest Shot: Single Biggest Sale
3. The Hotter Shot: Most Improved
   One night each week have an activity that ties into the theme, for example:
- first week: get together for *hot* drinks after work
- second week: go out for *hot*, spicy food
- third week: rent a basketball court for an office game or have a darts competition to see who is the hottest shot at darts
- fourth week: have an office party after work to announce the weekly and monthly winners of the three categories.

Time

Hold over a one-month period

Resource

Decoration for the office around the theme 'Hot Shot'; Hot Shot certificates

Prize

Certificate and cash prizes

Benefit
- Helps build the team spirit
- Adds a sense of fun and spirit to the office
- Gives the sales team another reason to boost production

SOURCE   Anne McFadzean

CERTIFICATE
Awarded to

1 The Hot Shot: Best Weekly Production

_____

2 The Hottest Shot: Single Biggest Sale

_____

3 The Hotter Shot: Most Improved

_____

Ten More Competition Ideas

In hindsight, there is often a better way to run a competition. Here are a few tips from regular competition organizers.

1. As a prize, give people 'well days' off or time off instead of sick days. (Vicki Jeffery)

2. If you employ temporary staff, involve them in the competitions. (Vicki Jeffery)

3. If you have competitions frequently, vary them to keep up the interest and target different results so that different people have a chance to win. (Sandra Lau)

4. Let people decide whether or not they want to participate. (Sandra Lau)

5. In order to involve non-sales staff in a competition, have them team up with a sales person. Both win. (Judy Purdon)

6. Remember that prizes for competitions do not need to be big. Often the fun is in the game. Also more competitions can be held if the value of the prizes is kept down. (Sandra Lau)

7. During a competition in a call center, have 'middle of the road' music playing in the background. Classical music will make the sales people too relaxed. Heavy metal music will make them too tense. CDs and tapes become too boring. A radio station playing middle of the road music with occasional chat is just right. It creates some gentle sound interference to give sales people a sense of privacy as they make outbound or take inbound calls. This also helps to overcome 'call reluctance'. (Simon Petersen)

8. Give a motivational poster as a prize for a competition. Obtain a catalogue so that the sales people can choose one they find most inspiring. (Caroline Eyre)

9. Equip the telephone sales and customer service staff with mirrors on their desks so they can make constant 'smile checks'. Give a white board to each person, on which they can write in big letters their daily goals and cross them off as they accomplish them. (Ian Low)

10. Have a bell that each person rings every time a sale is made in the office to keep the energy up. (Ian Low)

4

The Fun FACTOR

Team Building

Colored Balloon Competition

For a great visual impact and to cheer up the office, nothing beats balloons. Used in the following way, they give everyone a gauge as to how their team is faring against the other teams.

Purpose

- To provide competition that is visual and fun between teams
- To encourage team members to work together

Method

Ask each team to pick a color or draw a color out of a hat. For the length of the competition, the team wears predominantly this color and decorates its work stations in this color.

Plan a sales competition for one week. Set a specific target for the products or services on which the teams will be competing. Divide the target by ten. Each time a team reaches one-tenth of its target, the team members fill a colored balloon with helium gas and let it float up to the ceiling above the team. As the teams look around, they can see how other teams are progressing. This inspires teams to strive harder and send up more balloons.

Organize prizes for the team that reached the target first, the team that sold the most above target and a 'booby prize' for the team that came last.

Time

Great fun for one week

Resource

Balloons and helium gas

Reward

Various team awards and a prize for each member that costs about $10 to $20, wrapped in gift paper that is the color of their team

Benefit

- Creates a fun team competition that boosts morale
- Shows people what they are capable of achieving when team members work together

SOURCE   Chris Guinn

The Monthly Team Award

The manager of an in-house sales department asked his team how they would like to be rewarded for meeting targets. This is what they came up with. They have been using it successfully to achieve targets.

Purpose

- To empower the teams to meet and exceed their monthly target
- To allow a team to determine the individual contribution expected of each team member

Method

Each team in the center is given the same performance target to achieve. The team leader and members of the team meet to discuss the percentage of this target that should be met by each individual within the team. The decision would be based on several factors, for example:

1. last month's production
2. length of time in the job
3. hours of work
4. other responsibilities.

At the end of the month the team that has achieved the most over budget wins the monthly team award—a plaque with the name of the team inscribed on it, which sits on the team leader's desk for the month. There are also individual awards for first, second and third place for each team member's performance over budget.

Time

Hold for one month a year, or as required

Resource

An inscribed plaque

Reward

$200 meal voucher for the winning team to eat at a restaurant of its choice; a plaque and certificates for the first, second, and third place winners

Benefit

- Draws on the individual strengths of the team
- Encourages a supportive environment

SOURCE Alex Harper

Pizza Pizzazz

This is a fun, easy way to get everyone focused and involved on a limited budget. It achieves immediate results and is enjoyed by everyone in the office.

Purpose

- To boost the total daily production

Method

Set a daily target that is considered achievable but above average. Draw a big circle on paper or a white board that represents a pizza and mark it with eight segments. Place it in a prominent position for everyone to see.

Each time the sales team reaches one-eighth of the daily goal, ask one of the sales team members to color a pizza segment. When the goal is achieved and the whole pizza circle is colored in, send out for pizza for the whole team.

Time

Great fun one day a quarter, or as required

Resource

Paper or white board; markers

Reward

Pizza for all

Benefit

- Gives everyone an extra reason to exceed the daily goal
- Helps people realize that they can always beat their usual target

SOURCE   Louise Betts

The **Tube** Challenge

Staff will be talking about this game for months! It creates much hilarity as staff members try to carry a handful of styrofoam balls across the office. The styrofoam sticks to everything! Your office will be buzzing.

Purpose

- To stimulate the whole team to focus on reaching a daily goal
- To create energy, excitement and laughter

Method

Find a tall, large, clear plastic, hollow cylinder that can be displayed easily for all to see. Buy a large bag of small styrofoam balls that are used for packing or filling bean bags. Put the plastic cylinder and the bag of styrofoam balls at opposite ends of the room.

Each time a team member makes a sale, that person goes to the bag, picks up a handful of styrofoam balls, carries them across the room and puts them in the tube. The balls create lots of static electricity. This adds to the fun and hilarity because they are not easy to carry and they stick to people's hands.

As the cylinder fills, the sales people can see the team heading towards and passing its goal for the day.

At the end of the day, have a drinks and snacks party to congratulate each other.

Time

Great fun once a quarter

Resource

Plastic cylinder, styrofoam, drinks and snacks, vacuum cleaner

Reward

Fun

Benefit

- Provides a visual display of the team's achievements
- Gets the team members working together towards a common goal

SOURCE Sandi Einstein

Express Yourself

Why not use the creativity or musical talents of your employees to create a theme song for your office? The team at DHL Telesales in Melbourne won the Call Center of the Year Award for their state for two years in a row. To celebrate they created their own team song, and with their winnings they printed shirts with their slogan 'Express Yourself', the company name and their accomplishments.

Purpose

- To compose a theme song and slogan for your office or retail outlet
- To create a sense of pride and belonging to the organization

Method

Select a song that reflects something about the culture of your office or retail outlet. For example, an express freight company chose Madonna's 'Express Yourself' as its 'theme song'. The staff express themselves every day over the phone to customers and they sell express freight delivery.

A slogan can be chosen and printed on shirts for the staff to wear.

Time

Tie in this idea to celebrate a special event or promotion

Resource

Shirts to be printed with the slogan

Benefit

- Brings the group together to focus on a common goal
- Adds to the spirit of the group

SOURCE Jenni Swistak

The **Three 'P'** Teams

This is a way to use the different abilities, strengths and on-the-job experiences of all of your staff members. It will help keep them interested as they provide feedback and recommendations to management.

Purpose

- To utilize the various talents and skills of team members in areas other than customer service and sales
- To recognize the individual differences of your team members

Method

Divide team members into three groups based on their work experience, interests and abilities. Alternatively, they could choose the group they will join.

The three 'P' teams are as follows:

Procedure team: Responsible for quality assurance recommendations. The question they are always asking is: 'How can we do things better?'

Product team: Responsible for watching the stock levels. They advise the other team members, chase up back orders, suggest alternative products and liaise with the marketing department and the warehouse.

Proactive sales team: Responsible for liaising with marketing. When new products are introduced, they discuss ways to sell the products over the phone or over the counter. They will also give marketing valuable feedback on customer reactions to products and promotions.

Time

Ongoing responsibilities

Benefit

- Improves overall service to customers
- Improves operation of the office, retail outlet or call center

SOURCE   Yvonne Byrne

The Buddy Back-Up

There is nothing more frustrating for a customer or manager than not being able to reach the person they need. The Buddy Back-Up system provides another source of reference for them.

Purpose

- To provide team members with a back-up system when they are away from their desks, absent or on holiday

Method

Each team member should select a buddy. This person will have responsibility for:
1. looking after each other's clients when one of the buddies is unavailable
2. providing support, problem solving and product information
3. helping, in a sales environment, to encourage each other to reach targets.

When both buddies achieve their targets or deadline, recognition or rewards may be given as a team.

Time

An ongoing system

Reward

Certificates for the 'Buddies of the Month'

Benefit

- Ensures customers are looked after
- Helps to encourage cooperative behavior
- Provides another form of incentive activity in a sales environment
- Gives a sense of personal satisfaction

SOURCE   Vicki Jeffery

BUDDIES of the MONTH

Congratulations to _____

and _____

Photo

Photo

The Team Point Game

This is a great team-building game that can be adapted to almost any office or sale situation. Staff will learn to appreciate and encourage each other through their mutual dependence.

Purpose

- To increase sales through team cooperation and working for a common goal
- To reinforce positive behavior such as being punctual
- To create a fun and lively atmosphere within the office
- To create an appreciation between sales, customer service, support and administration staff for the assistance they give to one another

Method

Divide the office into teams by drawing names randomly out of a hat. However, make sure that each team has the same ratio of support and administration people to sales and customer service people. Each team then selects its own team leader and a team name.

With the input of the staff, devise a points system for a team point game. Points could be awarded for a variety of behaviors or accomplishments that are considered important in the office. These should include sales, customer service and support staff activities. The team can also lose points for negative behavior, such as coming to work late.

Keep track of the points each day. An artistic member of staff could design a chart to keep track of the daily and weekly results of each team. Display it prominently for all to see.

At the end of each week, the team with the most points wins a weekly prize. At the end of the competition the team with the most points wins the grand prize. There could also be individual prizes for the sales person with the highest conversion rate, the support staff member with the most points and the team leader with the most points.

Time

Hold weekly for six weeks

Resource

Wall chart for recording points

Prize   Weekly award: breakfast together at a local cafe; Grand prize: dinner at a five-star restaurant; Individual prizes: baskets of 'goodies'

Benefit
- Achieves an overall increase in sales for a small investment
- Helps to reinforce professional behavior
- Encourages a positive form of peer pressure
- Provides fun and friendly competition
- Promotes team building

SOURCE   Judy Purdon

Trainer's Notes:

The [Team] Champion

Tap into the expertise in the office! If you don't have experts in all areas, this is a great way to develop them. It is very satisfying for a staff member to be recognized as an expert in their field of accomplishment and to be able to share that expertise with others.

Purpose

- To encourage each person in the team to become an expert in one area

Method

Certain people in each team can be given recognition as experts in particular areas, such as:
1. product knowledge
2. complaint handling
3. sales expertise.

When team members have a question or a problem in a particular area, they can go to that team champion for help or advice.

Time

Make this a permanent system

Resource

Continuous training for the team champions in their area of expertise

Reward

Personal status as a team champion; certificate (example on page 97)

Benefit

- Utilizes people's strengths
- Helps new trainees to approach staff for advice

SOURCE   Rick Barrett

Team Champion

This is to certify that

_____

has achieved the level of
Team Champion
in

_____

Self-Directed Teams

What a great way to delegate! This could be a solution for the managers who take too much on their shoulders.

Purpose

- To give responsibility for setting and achieving goals to the individuals within a team

Method

Each team within the office becomes a self-directed team. This means that the team has the responsibility for:
1. setting its own targets
2. monitoring behavior
3. working within its own budget
4. setting timetables
5. appointing its own team leader.

Management assists the teams by giving them all the relevant information to make a decision. Management acts as a facilitator, rather than a dictator, in helping the teams to set their objectives.

There is no competition between the teams. Teams are encouraged to review their outcomes every three to six months.

Benefit

- Gives responsibility back to the team
- Helps to change behavior

SOURCE   Ron James

Trainer's Notes:

The `Focus` Group

The staff members who deal with customers or systems every day have the best ideas on what the customer wants or needs and what works. Why not tap into their expertise? This method has been used very successfully.

Purpose

- To receive valuable feedback from the staff in a variety of areas

Method

From time to time, invite staff members to be part of a focus group. The focus groups may be led by the company trainer, the product manager, the project team leader or the sales manager.

The selected staff members are asked to bring to the focus group their thoughts, ideas or suggestions on a topic of concern. Each member of the group should write their ideas on a Post-it note or slip of paper. These notes are then displayed on a white board for points of conversation. This will prevent the 'talkers' from dominating the discussion.

Some of the topics for your focus group might be:
1. marketing and sales ideas
2. reaction to a proposed advertising campaign
3. work flow
4. systems
5. training.

Time

One hour per session, up to four sessions

Resource

Meeting room, Post-it notes

Benefit

- Allows different perspectives to be considered
- Injects valuable customer front-line input
- Provides a valuable reality check

SOURCE   Carol York

We **Both** Win

This is a great way to encourage your staff to persuade customers to enter your competitions. When the customer wins, the staff member who helped them wins a prize as well.

Purpose

- To encourage the sales people to persuade customers to participate in a competition

Method

During a special promotion or competition for customers, offer a corresponding prize for the sales person who sells to a winning customer. Always let the sales person be the one to tell the customer of their win.

Time

For the duration of a competition or promotion for customers

Prize

Bottle of wine, movie tickets

Benefit

- Gives the sales person an extra reason to sell
- Develops a closer bond between the sales person and the customer

SOURCE   Sandra Lau

Trainer's Notes:

Five **Team** Get-Togethers

After-hours get-togethers are one of the best team-building exercises. Below are examples of what works for three different managers.

Purpose

- To give teams a chance to discuss relevant work issues
- To allow staff to get together and enjoy each other's company

Method

Here are five ways for different teams to get together:

1. At 4.30 every Friday, break up for a glass of champagne. It's a great chance to 'let off steam' and end the week on a positive note. (Vicki Jeffery)

2. Every two to three months, ask everyone to stay back for a meeting with management. This gives management a chance to go over future plans and provides an opportunity to praise performance. It is also a suitable venue to ask staff for suggestions. It can lead to an overall improvement in team atmosphere. Afterwards, the company then takes everyone out to dinner. (Pat Caton)

3. Have a wine tasting after work. Ask everyone to bring a bottle of their favorite wine. The company provides crackers and cheese. (Bob Westcott)

4. Have a monthly lunchtime meeting with half the staff at a time. Take this opportunity to discuss all housekeeping matters then have a guest speaker to speak on a subject that is relevant to the group. (Bob Westcott)

5. Pep up a dreary day. Get everyone to chip in a few dollars for lunch and order pizza or another popular food that can be delivered for lunch. (Vicki Jeffery)

Time

Set aside one lunch break or an hour or two after work, when a need arises

Benefit

- Adds interest to the day
- Builds the team spirit
- Allows staff to interact without distractions

SOURCE   As given above

Team **Night Out**

Make the team night out a night to remember! Ideas for fun group outings are endless. These activities will create good feelings that will carry over into the workplace.

Purpose

- To allow team members to get to know each other outside the office
- To develop a sense of friendship and mutual appreciation

Method

Encourage team members to organize a team night out once every two months. Management may contribute a small donation towards the event to encourage participation. Some examples of events that are a lot of fun include:

1. bowling
2. theme restaurant
3. line dancing
4. horseback riding
5. card party at a team member's house.

Time

Once every two months

Benefit

- Improves office communication
- Helps people to see each other in another light
- Encourages cooperation
- Builds esprit de corps

SOURCE   Caroline Eyre

Trainer's Notes:

Team Slogan Week

The creativity of staff members when put to a challenge can be amazing. Here are a few slogans that were created in a customer service department of a cosmetics company in Sydney, Australia.

Purpose

- To encourage team members to work together
- To focus on exceptional customer service
- To build self-esteem

Method

Team Slogan Week is a time for teams to celebrate what they stand for as professionals in customer service. Each team is asked to come up with a slogan expressing the team's philosophy of exceptional customer service. Here are some examples:

1. *Enjoy your customers and they will enjoy you.*
2. *When the going gets tough, we are the right stuff.*
3. *Service with a smile.*
4. *Always above and beyond the call of duty.*

Give the teams banner paper, felt pens and decorative materials to design a banner that they will display for the week. Photograph the teams with the banners and encourage everyone to display the photos later on their desks as a constant reminder.

Time

Hold over a one-week period

Resource

Banner materials, camera, and a photo holder for every person in which they can put the photograph of their team holding the banner

Benefit

- Encourages teamwork
- Acts as a reinforcement for exceptional customer service

SOURCE   Carolyn Greenwich

Bat and Ball Competition

Everyone responds to a team sport competition! You don't even need a prize! Playing and winning create fun and increase sales results. This game has been used successfully in an outbound call center. Have fun adapting the idea to your work situation.

Purpose

- To improve the effective call rate in the outbound sales environment
- To create interest and fun in the day

Method

A cricket game is the basis for this team participation activity but it can easily be adapted to become a baseball game if this is more popular with the staff.

Divide the group into two teams of even numbers. One side will start 'bowling' and the other side will start 'batting'. Each team is named after a favorite local or professional team and the players' names are posted on the wall.

Decide what is an 'effective call', that is, how many of these calls each person should make in an hour. This will become the effective call rate for the cricket or baseball game.

The batting side

Each effective call made by a team member on the batting side counts as one run. In each hour, if every team member meets the effective call rate, the team gets an additional four runs. Every sale counts as six runs.

Each hour, count the runs made by the batting team and display the results prominently.

The bowling side

The bowling side also determines its wickets by the effective call rate. For each hour that the team averages the effective call rate, it gets a 'wicket', and removes one of the names of the other team's players from the list on the wall. When the team achieves a certain number of sales, it also gets a wicket and removes a name from the team list. When all the players are 'out', the bowling team goes in to bat and the other team bowls.

Time

Great fun held over two days to one week

Resource
Score-keeping poster displayed for everyone to see

Prize
No prizes—the fun is in the game

Benefit
- Raises the effective call rate
- Helps overcome call reluctance

SOURCE Stephen Jones

Trainer's Notes:

The **Grand Prix**

This is a game for an inbound or outbound call center. A great time to play is during the Grand Prix or the Indianapolis 500. This may sound a little complicated, but that's the fun!

Purpose
- To increase the effective call rate
- To reach targets and have fun as a team

Method

Divide the group into two or more teams of even numbers. Each team picks a name for its Formula One car.

Determine an effective call rate per hour (the number of outbound or inbound calls per hour for each sales or customer service staff member). Each hour of work per team member represents the equivalent of one lap of the track.

Each team is automatically given 8 seconds as a lap time to start. For every effective call over the target call rate, the team receives minus 0.07 seconds. For every call under the effective call rate the team is given plus 0.07 seconds. A bonus of 0.07 seconds could be added for every sale.

Determine how many laps (hours of the competition) you will work. Thirty-eight laps will take one week, 76 laps will take two weeks. Devise a fun and visually effective way of showing the progress of the cars.

Time

Hold over a one- or two-week period

Resource

Poster material to track the results

Prize

Team trophy, bottle of champagne for the winning team

Benefit
- Creates a sense of team fun while making outbound and inbound calls
- Creates mutual encouragement

SOURCE Stephen Jones

The **Thermometer**

Why just buy another amenity for the staff room when you can let the staff have the fun of winning it and really appreciating it? This game will show you how!

Purpose
- Creates a common goal for the whole team or office to reach and be rewarded

Method

Find out or ask staff to vote for something that the whole office would really appreciate as an addition to the staff room. It could be a microwave, a television or magazine subscriptions, for example. Then arrange for the staff to earn what they wish for, as follows.

Set a certain target or deadline that they must achieve. The target or deadline needs to be realistic yet considered above the norm. Have one of the more creative members of staff draw the outline of a large thermometer on paper. Display this so that it can be easily seen by everyone. Each day, as the office achieves a certain level of progress towards the target or deadline, color in an appropriate portion of the thermometer.

If the target is reached in the allotted time period of the game, the staff are rewarded with their selected addition to the staff room.

Time

Use this over one to two months

Resource

Material to display thermometer visually

Prize

The item for which the staff vote as being a desirable addition to the staff room

Benefit
- Pulls everyone together by working for a common goal
- Makes the addition to the staff room more appreciated because the staff earned it themselves

SOURCE   Soula Skliros

The **Q Card** Game

The staff of this insurance company are still talking about this game. It is great for office situations where staff have lots of routine and repetitive activities. This will liven the place up!

Purpose

- To encourage team work
- To improve product knowledge
- To build staff morale

Method

The Q Card game is a combination of a treasure hunt, Trivial Pursuit, and Snakes and Ladders. Although this game is intricate, this adds to the fun and excitement.

Divide the office into four teams by picking names at random out of a hat. Everyone in the office is involved, including sales, customer service, support and administration staff. Each team picks a ridiculous name and mascot, such as Cool Cats, Bums, Smart Asses or Dumbos.

The game involves various steps with the ultimate team objective to reach the finish line on the Snakes and Ladders board.

The first step: Each day the Q Card (the question card) is hidden somewhere in the office. To find the Q Card, team members need to watch for a cryptic clue on their e-mail. In order to find the Q Card they need to solve the clue that leads to its location. The team that is first to find the Q Card goes on to the next step.

The second step: The winning team then throws the dice on the Trivial Pursuit board to find out its category. The categories range from product knowledge, sport and movies to other areas of interest to the group. The team then has ten minutes to come up with an answer to the question. If the question is answered correctly, the team moves on to the next step.

The third step: The team now throws the dice to move its position on the Snakes and Ladders board. A personalized Snakes and Ladders board can be made that gives bonus prizes, booby prizes, an extra throw, or tells the player to move back spaces instead of moving forward. This adds extra fun and intrigue to the game.

The team that reaches the top of the Snakes and Ladders board is declared the winner.

Time   Hold over a period of about one to two months

Resource   Material to make a Snakes and Ladders board and dice

Prize   Keep the prize a secret. Make all the staff winners by having a picnic in the park for everyone complete with a barbecue. For those members of the winning team provide a little extra, such as a gift basket with a company T-shirt, champagne, movie tickets and chocolates.

Benefit   • Creates a win-win concept
     • Reinforces team playing
     • Boosts morale

SOURCE   Judy Purdon

Building Blocks to Success

This game will help the office to boost their sales figures significantly. It is a creative, visual, back-to-childhood game that staff love and respond to with enthusiasm.

Purpose

- To put focus on selling a specific range of products
- To increase sales
- To energize the team

Method

1. Divide the group into teams of between two and eight people. Provide enough Lego pieces so that each group can eventually make up a model, such as a car, an animal or whatever appeals to the group's sense of fun. If possible use the larger block sets for greater visual impact.
2. Start the game by announcing that, for each sale the team makes, it wins a piece of Lego to add to its creation of a model. Another alternative is to award different colors of Lego to different products, or to give multiple pieces depending on the dollar amount of the sale.
3. As soon as the first team builds its Lego model, the competition is over. In order to track the performance of each person in the office, display a personal poster. Each time a sale is made by the sales person, place a rectangular or square sticker in the shape of building blocks on their 'Building Blocks to Success' poster. Use different colored stickers that designate different values or types of sales.
4. At the end of the team competition, the person with the most building blocks wins the individual prize.

Time

Hold this over approximately one month

Resource

Lego sets, poster paper, colored stickers

Prize

A special lunch for the winning team; a $50 gift voucher for the individual winner

Benefit

- Consolidates team work
- Reduces stress
- Gives a change from the normal routine
- Allows some back-to-childhood fun

SOURCE   Jann Fenley

Trainer's Notes:

The **Football** Match

This game is so popular in one of the phone centers of an Australian bank that it has been introduced to all the other centers. It can be adapted for other office or retail situations. It is fun for sports fans and everyone involved.

Purpose

- To stimulate sales production
- To create a sense of team spirit

Method

Divide the office or call center into teams for this game or use the teams that are already in place. Select the name of a football team that each team wants to represent.

If the number of teams is sufficient, form a league and organize an official 'draw'. During the course of the regular football season, the teams should have the opportunity to play the football sales game with each of the other teams once or twice. Display a results ladder so that the teams know exactly how they are ranked during the season.

The games take place during the busiest part of each day. Each game lasts for two hours with a 'half time' break after the first hour. During the game, each sale or group of sales made by the members of a team represents a try or touchdown or field goal depending on the type or amount of the sale. As the game continues, the score is flashed up on a monitor or written up on a board for all the sales people to see. At the end of the game, the team with the most points wins, and the sales person who has sold the most is named Player of the Match.

Towards the end of the season, hold the 'play offs' with the top four teams competing in the finals for a place in the Grand Final or Call Center Bowl.

Time

Each game lasts for two hours and all teams play each other once or twice during the season

Prize

Trophy inscribed with the team name

Benefit

- Creates a sense of excitement
- Picks up the tempo of the office or call center
- Adds interest to the day for the sales people
- Increases sales

SOURCE Trevor Williams

The Six Weekly Business Plan

This is a great way to keep staff involved and focused on a short-term department goal from start to finish. They will take ownership and pride in contributing to the team effort.

Purpose

- To create a focus on the common goal of the office, retail outlet or call center
- To involve the team in achieving a result even though there is no individual financial reward

Method

Hold a meeting every six weeks with the team or the entire staff to discuss the business plan for the next six weeks and outline the financial objectives of this plan. Discuss specific sales campaigns in detail, including ways to approach the campaigns and any problems that may be encountered.

With this information at hand, the sales and customer service people have a better idea of what they need to do and how to do it. Supervisors should keep an open-door policy during campaigns so that they stay close to staff and know what is affecting them positively and negatively.

At the end of four weeks, bring the team or staff together again for a meeting to discuss how they are all progressing. If they are on target, congratulate them and encourage their continued success. If they are behind target, encourage discussion on what they need to do to reach the target in the next two weeks.

Time

Hold every six weeks

Reward

Get together at the end of each six-week business cycle for drinks and snacks and give lots of verbal praise and appreciation

Benefit

- Involves teams or staff in the 'big picture'
- Helps people to take ownership of their contribution to the business objectives of the office, retail outlet or call center
- Allows efforts to be assessed and noted for salary review time

SOURCE   Danielle Murrie

You Are Number 1

This is a great way to make your staff feel special. Some will be able to relive the feeling of the locker room pep talk, while others will enjoy that experience for the first time.

Purpose

- To build team spirit
- To develop the analogy between sports teams and office teams
- To reward the team at the end of a project or budget period

Method

1. Rent the function room of a favorite sports team for a team dinner. Many such rooms are under-utilized in the off-season or the middle of the week.
2. When everyone arrives have them gather in the team's locker room. Give them team shirts with their name and the number 1 on the back.
3. When everyone is assembled, give a locker room 'motivation talk'. Use it as an opportunity to say 'thank you'.
4. Give everyone an opportunity to throw the ball around on the field.

Time

Great fun when held one evening, a couple of times a year

Resource

Budget for dinner and team shirts

Benefit

- Provides an evening to remember
- Makes everyone feel special and appreciated
- Builds self-esteem

SOURCE   Catherine De Vrye

The Office Video

Many people love to see themselves on film. Whether the video is taken by a professional or by an office amateur, it will create excitement and good feelings.

Purpose

- To create a sense of pride and belonging in the office, retail outlet or call center
- To create a training tool for all new employees to the company so they understand the purpose and function of the area being videoed
- To show attendees at the company's conference what other departments do

Method

Hire a professional video maker or find someone within the team who has the talent to put a video together. The professional video can show the department and the staff at work, explaining the objectives and accomplishments of the department.

A second video could be presented in a more light-hearted manner, with staff emphasizing the humorous and stressful moments of the job.

Time

This takes approximately one month to complete

Resource

Budget for a professional video, or the assistance of a person willing to film it on a 'shoestring' budget

Benefit

- Helps to make everyone feel special
- Acknowledges their importance within the company
- Allows a form of self-congratulation

SOURCE   Jenni Swistak

The Team Sales Swap

This is an unusual way to perk up sales staff. It encourages staff to help each other and to achieve better sales results.

Purpose
- To increase sales
- To help sales staff to think about people other than themselves
- To encourage the application of new sales techniques

Method

One day once a month, pair up each sales person with another sales person of similar sales ability. On that day they will sell for each other. Whatever sale one person in the pair generates, the other person gets the commission or credit for it. The exception to this rule would be any extremely large sale that happens to come in on that day.

The pairing of the sales people creates exceptional teamwork. They could go for a run together, make sure they eat a healthy breakfast and offer encouragement and sales ideas to each other during the day.

Time

Hold this one day every month

Reward

The sales person whose sales are lower than the other can make up the difference with a drink after work or a lunch out

Benefit
- Improves time management drastically
- Increases sales
- Helps build team spirit

SOURCE Sandy Perrett

Personality Styles

Many people love personality-style training. Linda Urquhart, one of the leading keynote speakers and trainers in the United States, provides the tools to run your own personality-style workshop.

Purpose

- To build team spirit
- To help people understand the differences in personality styles
- To tailor customer service and sales styles to a customer's individual style

Method

1. Introduce to team members the concept of the four dominant personality styles by reading the introduction and style descriptions provided on pages 120–21.

2. Invite team members to take the quiz, 'What color are you?' on pages 122–23.

3. Each person should add up the number of ticks under each style to identify the color in which they are strongest—blue, red, green or yellow. Provide blue, red, green, and yellow dots for team members to place on their name tags or use colored pens to draw them.

4. Team members should now form groups, and brainstorm, for about five minutes each, the following 'What do we have in common?' questions. Each group should record its answers on a flip chart using colored pens.

   ### Questions
   (a) What is important to us, and what brings us joy?
   (b) What are our strong points and what are our best qualities?
   (c) What bugs us, or what 'pushes our button'?

5. Each group should now report its answers to these questions to the other groups. Encourage everyone to be involved and to take notes.

6. Form the color groups again. Ask each group to analyze how they think another style would like to be treated. Have the blue group and the red group analyze each other, and the greens and yellows analyze each other. Use these questions:

Questions

How would you best deal with a person from the other color style to:

(a) resolve that person's complaint?

(b) buy a product or use a service?

(c) support a position?

7. Continue with the discussion and allow each group to present its findings. Give the other color group the 'right of reply' to see if they got it right.

Time

This takes approximately one hour

Resource

Red, blue, green and yellow sticky dots; four flip charts; four sets of colored pens

Benefit

- Helps people to understand why they sometimes have difficulty developing rapport with a customer
- Provides a valuable sales and customer service tool for staff
- Helps people appreciate the diversity in all of us

SOURCE   Linda Urquhart

Trainer's Notes:

119

Introducing the Four Styles

The concept of personality styles has been around for centuries. Around 400 BC, Hippocrates designated the four styles as sanguine, bile, phlegmatic and choleric. Carl Jung led a resurgence in style popularity in the early twentieth century, calling them the thinker, feeler, intuitive and analyzer. Many more ideas have been published and all fit into four basic categories.

Each of us develops our own unique style that works for us. As children we tried out different behaviors and kept the ones that got us the results we thought we wanted. Even now, if we appreciate a certain behavior in others we often try to incorporate it into our own style. Some of us are more assertive, some more 'laid back'. Some tend to be more task-oriented, others more people-oriented.

We have given each personality style a color. Take a moment to read the descriptions of the four colors below.

Style I: Blue

Blue is the color of the sky and the ocean. Explorers have long been pioneers on the ocean and in space and their characteristics match this style. They enjoy looking at the 'big picture', being in charge and are comfortable taking risks. They are goal-oriented and like to have their finger in many pots. They are motivated by challenge and competition. People of other 'styles' get frustrated with these 'blues' because they see them as impatient, abrupt and selective listeners, but they appreciate their strong leadership qualities.

Style II: Red

Red is the color of blood and Valentines, and tends to connote passion and enthusiasm, which sounds a lot like the reds. Reds are happiest when they are influencing or entertaining other people. They, like the blues, are comfortable taking risks and enjoy trying new things. They get bored if they have to do the same old thing all the time. They are the charming, playful, spontaneous, talkative types who are energized by being the center of attention. They are motivated by recognition—they want to be liked! Other styles see them as unfocused procrastinators who make up the rules as they go along, but appreciate their talents as great promoters who can sell anything.

☞ Reproduced from *The Fun Factor: Games, sales contests and activities that make work fun and get results*
Text © 1997 Carolyn Greenwich. Design and illustration © 1997 McGraw-Hill Book Co Australia Pty Ltd

Style III: Green

Green is the color of the American dollar and was one of the original colors of computer screens. Greens are the most comfortable of all the styles where accuracy and numbers are important. Perfectionism is inherent in their style. 'If a job's worth doing, it's worth doing right—the first time' might be their motto. They are willing to take the time to get the job done right. They are the best of the four styles at critical thinking and planning. They make the best administrators as they like order, structure, following guidelines and plans (especially if they orientate them). Other styles complain that the greens are too rigid, too slow at making a decision, too 'picky', but value their planning and problem-solving skills.

Style IV: Yellow

Yellow is the color of the sun and yellows are like a ray of sunshine when they enter a room with their warm and caring style. Family is their number one priority. They tend to be most concerned with the needs of others. They are the best team builders, always listening to, encouraging and bringing out the best in others. They are motivated by appreciation for work done and have a strong need to please others. Like the greens, they dislike confrontation and will give in to others to avoid conflict. Other styles see yellows as too soft, not hard-nosed enough, indecisive (they can see all sides of an issue) and resistant to change. They are often the 'glue' that holds a group together.

☞ Reproduced from *The Fun Factor: Games, sales contests and activities that make work fun and get results*

Text © 1997 Carolyn Greenwich. Design and illustration © 1997 McGraw-Hill Book Co Australia Pty Ltd

What Color Are You?
A Quiz about Personality Styles

Tick the characteristics that best describe you.

Style I—Blue
____Decisive
____Independent
____Tends to be dominant
____Strong willed
____Wants immediate results
____Causes action
____Likes power and authority
____Likes freedom from control
____Dislikes supervision
____Outspoken
____Wants direct answers
____Restless
____Competitive
____Adventurous
____Assertive

Style II—Red
____Optimistic
____Tends to be exciting/stimulating
____Generates enthusiasm
____Often dramatic
____Talkative
____Open and friendly
____Likes working with people
____Likes participating in groups
____Desires to help others
____Wants freedom of expression
____Wants freedom from detail
____Likes change, spontaneity
____Persuasive
____Appears confident
____Likes recognition

(continued)

Style III—Green
____Orderly
____Performs exacting work
____Likes controlled circumstances
____Likes assurance of security
____Uses critical thinking
____Follows rules
____Reads and follows instructions
____Prefers status quo
____Dislikes sudden or abrupt change
____Tends to be serious and persistent
____Cautious
____Diplomatic
____Respectful
____Agreeable
____Checks for accuracy

Style IV—Yellow
____Patient
____Accommodating
____Good listener
____Shows loyalty
____Concentrates on task accuracy
____Likes security and stability
____Needs good reasons for change
____Home life a priority
____Expects credit for work done
____Likes traditional procedures
____Dislikes conflict
____Neighborly
____Considerate towards others
____Important to perform good work
____Pleasure in sharing and giving

Under which color do most of your ticks occur? This is your dominant personality style.

The **Fruit** Sale

Are you sick of candy and chocolate? This is a fun team game that is healthy too! It is great for a small budget, because the losing team provides the prize!

Purpose

- To encourage better sales results through a fun, friendly team competition
- To display the teams' progress towards their targets

Method

Divide the sales people into two teams. If the office, retail outlet or call center has several teams, then have two teams at a time challenge each other.

Make up colorful cut-outs of pieces of fruit. If the company has a day care center attached, this would be a great activity for the children.

Hang a long streamer from the ceiling for each team, with a basket of the cut-out fruit pieces nearby. Every time a team member makes a sale, they get to pin a piece of fruit on the streamer. At the end of the day or week, the team displaying the most pieces of fruit wins. Each member from the losing team has to bring in a piece of fruit to make up a large fruit platter for the winning team's morning tea break.

Time

Great fun held over one day to one week

Resource

Paper for fruit cut-outs, streamers

Prize

A beautiful fruit platter provided by the losing team

Benefit

- Builds the team spirit
- Puts the focus on sales results

SOURCE   Christine Apoleski; Nada Simovski

5

The Fun FACTOR

Optimize Training

The KEYS to the Customer

How often do staff think of the customer from only one perspective? This is a great training tool to help staff put together the total picture of their customers: their Knowledge, Expectations, Yearnings and Situation.

Purpose

- To provide a useful training tool for use in sales/training meetings
- To help sales and customer service staff to understand their customers better
- To encourage sales and customer service staff to come up with helpful questions to ask their customers

Method

When staff understand the 'KEYS' to their customer, they find it easier to sell their product or service to that customer. KEYS is an acronym for four different types of questions they could ask or information they could obtain by listening to the prospective customer.

Sales and customer service staff could be asked to suggest information that would be useful to obtain through listening or asking questions in each of the four 'KEYS' areas. Then they could devise questions that they would feel comfortable asking. Some examples are given below.

K for Knowledge—general or specific information about the customer and the degree of customer's knowledge about the product or service.

Sample questions
Have you used a similar product in the past?
How familiar are you with our range of services?

E for Expectation—what are the prospective customer's expectations of the services or products?

Sample questions
Do you have any special requirements?
What changes would you like to see from your current supplier?
Why do you need this product or service?

(continued)

Y for Yearnings—determine what is the best way to assist this customer.

Sample questions
Does this customer want me to be quick, friendly, supportive or a provider of information?
How can I exceed the customer's expectations?
What is the best type of closing question I can ask?

S for Situation—the how, when, where and what questions that most sales people know they must ask.

Sample questions
How many do you need?
When do you want to make a decision?
Where will you use the product?
What exactly do you need it for?

Discuss the importance of finding out as much as possible about the customer. Then brainstorm ways to improve the questions that staff members are already asking. Create new questions to use in the sales process. Role play these questions to see how they 'feel'.

Ask the staff members to start using the new questions. In the next sales training meeting, ask for feedback.

Time

Takes about one to two hours

Resource

Handout sheet with a description of the 'KEYS' (see page 129)

Benefit

- Helps to improve the questioning techniques of the sales and customer service staff
- Improves their understanding of the customers
- Makes it easier for the sales and customer service staff to sell

SOURCE   Carolyn Greenwich

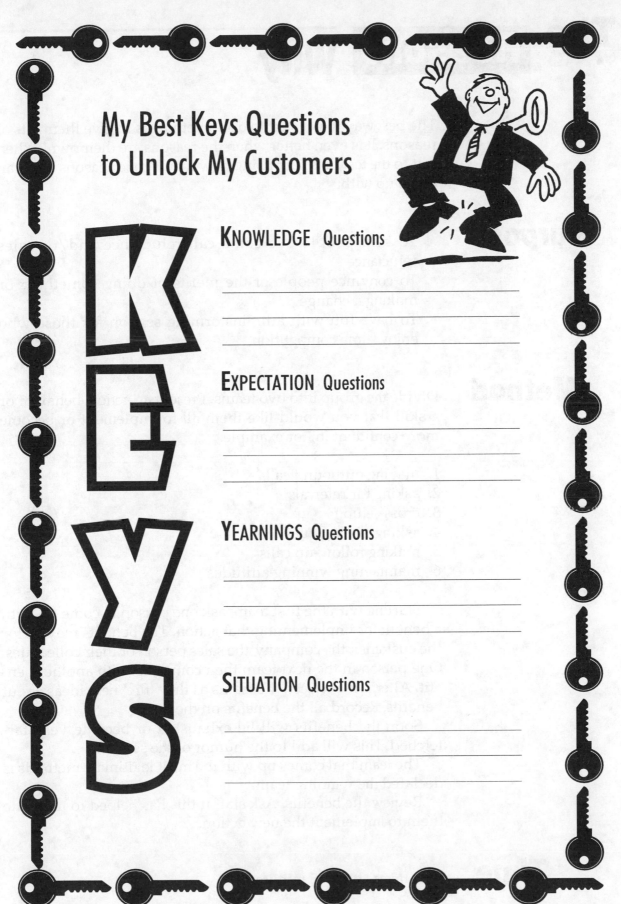

My Best Keys Questions to Unlock My Customers

KEYS

KNOWLEDGE Questions

_____
_____
_____

EXPECTATION Questions

_____
_____
_____

YEARNINGS Questions

_____
_____
_____

SITUATION Questions

_____
_____
_____

☞ Reproduced from _The Fun Factor: Games, sales contests and activities that make work fun and get results_
Text © 1997 Carolyn Greenwich. Design and illustration © 1997 McGraw-Hill Book Co Australia Pty Ltd

The Reasons Why

The best way to get staff to do something is to give them lots of reasons. It is even better when the reasons are their own! When put to the test, it is surprising how many good reasons staff can come up with.

Purpose

- To help people overcome call reluctance and/or sales reluctance
- To convince people of the merits of doing something or making a change
- To have fun with a brainstorming session for those who enjoy some competition

Method

Divide the group into two teams. Present an action, behavior or a skill that you would like them all to implement or become more confident in, for example:

1. making outbound calls
2. asking for referrals
3. cross-selling
4. asking closing questions
5. making follow-up calls
6. maintaining winning attitudes.

Starting with the first team, ask one person to come up with a benefit for implementing that action. The benefits may be for the customer, the company, the sales person or their colleagues. One person in the next team then comes up with another benefit. Alternate between the teams as they 'fire' new ideas about benefits. Record all the benefits on the board.

Soon the benefits will be exhausted or become very far-fetched. This will add to the humor of the session.

The team that comes up with the most legitimate methods is declared the winning team.

Review the benefits. Ask staff if this has helped to motivate them to implement the new action.

Time

This takes about 15 minutes

Resource	White board, markers
Reward	Candy bars for the winning team
Benefit	• Helps staff to understand the benefits of an action because they came up with 'The Reasons Why'
SOURCE	Carolyn Greenwich

Trainer's Notes:

The E-Mail Quiz

This quiz is a great way to maximize the office e-mail system and utilize the odd spare moments of the staff to improve their skills and knowledge.

Purpose

- To improve product knowledge, computer skills, and sales and customer service talents
- To determine in what areas training is needed

Method

Twice a month, devise an e-mail quiz that the staff can work on in quiet moments. Include a range of questions, for example:

1. multiple choice
2. definitions
3. limited response explanation
4. scenario response.

The staff are given a few days to enter their answers to the questions. When the quiz is finished, it is checked by the manager. The correct answers are posted on the e-mail.

Time

Hold this quiz twice a month

Resource

e-mail facilities

Benefit

- Improves knowledge and skills
- Helps to achieve better accuracy

SOURCE   Alex Harper

From Ballistic Babblers to Whinge Warriors

This is a tremendous way to get relief from being polite to rude customers! Staff will learn something new into the bargain.

Purpose

- To show staff how unproductive emotional reactions are to both internal and external customers
- To present effective complaint management techniques in a new way

Method

During a sales or customer service meeting, staff are introduced to two games: Ballistic Babblers and Whinge Warriors.

Ballistic Babblers

Staff are asked to form pairs. One will be the complaining customer and the other the complaint handler. They must sit back to back so they can only hear each other.

This is the scenario that they must act out.

> *You have just arrived at work in a terrible mood and have a throbbing headache. The first call of the day is from the 'customer from Hell' who 'lets you have it'. Instead of keeping your cool and acting professionally, act defensively and respond emotionally, breaking all the rules of complaint management.*

Give the partners four minutes for the role play, then switch roles. There will be lots of noise, 'letting off steam' and laughter.

Team members should discuss how they felt in each role and what, if anything, they accomplished.

Whinge Warriors

In pairs again and sitting back to back, team members are presented with this new scenario.

They are now going to be 'Whinge Warriors'.

> *You have been asked to feature in an educational video on how to handle an irate customer. Your task is to detach yourself emotionally yet to empathize with the customer and find a solution by doing the following.*

(continued)

1. Listen to the complaint without reacting emotionally or defensively.

2. Acknowledge the concern verbally to the customer.

3. Suggest a fair solution or educate the customer for future occasions (whatever is appropriate).

4. Reach a mutual agreement.

5. Thank the customer for bringing it to your attention.

Allow four minutes for each person to handle the complaint. When the role play is finished, have a general discussion on how they felt when playing the different roles. How difficult was it to remain emotionally removed from the verbal attack? How did the irate customers feel when they were listened to and acknowledged? What was the difference in the outcomes of the Ballistic Babbler exercise and the Whinge Warrior exercise?

Time

This takes about 45 minutes

Benefit

- Gives the staff a chance to 'let off steam'
- Reinforces the correct manner for handling a difficult customer

SOURCE Muffy McWhinnie

Trainer's Notes:

The Movie Message

Do you want to increase your customer satisfaction level? It went up significantly after the staff in this computer company were involved in this activity.

Purpose

- To stimulate ideas among the team on how to improve customer satisfaction
- To help the team become more market-driven

Method

Many movies have a customer service message that may stimulate your team to improve performance. For example, *Dead Poets Society* is about a teacher who could be said to be market-driven.

Provide movie tickets to team members and their partners to a movie that offers such a message. Ask them to come up with ideas from the movie that will help the team produce a higher level of customer satisfaction.

Hold a meeting after seeing the movie for everyone to present their ideas and how to implement them.

Time

One hour for meeting

Resource

Two movie tickets for each member of staff

Benefit

- Encourages new ideas to be put forward in a fun way
- Provides a way of saying thank you
- Lets staff know that management values their opinions

SOURCE Catherine De Vrye

What I **Learned** Today

Remember the magic circle from camp days? Why not apply this to the office? Everyone will learn and have fun at the same time.

Purpose

- To provide people with an opportunity to share their experiences
- To improve listening skills
- To build self-esteem

Method

At the end of the day, get everyone in the team together in a comfortable area. Arrange the chairs so that people sit facing each other in a circle.

Start with one person who says: 'What I learned today was …'. The next person then repeats what the first person said and adds their own sentence to it. Continue around the circle so that each person repeats what the people before them said.

The game can continue with:
'What made me happy today was …'
or 'What made me mad today was …'.

Time

This takes about one hour at the end of the day

Benefit

- Gives everyone a chance to vent their emotions
- Helps staff members understand each other
- Improves listening skills
- Builds team spirit

SOURCE Sandi Einstein

What Motivates You?

When is the last time management and staff had a good look at the many factors that both motivate and de-motivate them? This is a way to develop a clearer understanding.

Purpose

- To identify factors that will motivate sales, customer service, support and administrative staff
- To involve staff in the formation of motivation activities that appeal to the organization

Method

To help people do their very best and enjoy their jobs, it is important to understand what motivates and what de-motivates them. This exercise can be used to explore three sources of motivation—management, colleagues, and yourself.

Team members can do this individually or in small groups. Each person is given a sheet that asks questions about what motivates and hinders them (see page 139).

When everyone has completed the questions, have a group discussion to share the answers. Try to gain an overall picture.

Now ask the members of the group to come up with specific ideas or ways to motivate them. Offer suggestions or use activities from this book that seem suited to the group.

Time

This takes about one to two hours, depending on size of group

Resource

Training room, white board, and specially designed work sheets

Benefit

- Helps people to understand how others are motivated
- Stimulates the formation of motivation activities that will encourage the team to do its best
- Gives insight into how each person would like to be treated

SOURCE Carolyn Greenwich

Motivation by management

What helps?

....

....

What hinders?

....

....

Motivation by colleagues

What helps?

....

....

What hinders?

....

....

Motivation by yourself

What helps?

....

....

What hinders?

....

....

Word of the Week

This is a quick, easy and effective way to help implement a new skill or to reinforce a positive attitude. The words act as a visual and auditory prompt for staff.

Purpose

- To help staff to change their attitudes
- To help staff to improve their sales skills

Method

Select a word that represents something that needs to be changed or improved in the office. Words that could be selected might be 'Focus', 'Sell', 'Service', 'Care', 'Smile', 'Team'.

Ask the staff to come up with an acronym for the chosen word that describes how they are going to use the meaning of this word to change their attitudes or improve their sales. For example, if the word is 'FOCUS', the acronym could express ways to become more attentive to customers, as follows:

Friendly
Obliging
Courteous
Understanding
Sincere.

Staff can make their own signs with these words on them to display at their desks for the week. This sign will be a reminder and a reinforcement of the word.

At the end of the week, meet for drinks and a snack. Play a word game to continue the theme, such as a spelling bee or a dictionary game.

Time

Use this over the period of one week

Resource

Material to make the word signs

Prize

Small value prize for the word games

Benefit

- Gives people a fun way to decorate their work stations
- Creates a sense of unity and purpose

SOURCE   Carolyn Greenwich

Book Review

This is a great way to share the information in business books with a message that will help develop the staff members. This activity might even be the beginning of a business book library for the office.

Purpose

- To encourage staff to read books on sales, customer service, business or any area that would enhance their abilities
- To keep alive the spirit of continual improvement

Method

Provide each member of the team with a favorite business-related book. Either start a library of books or give each person a copy to keep.

Ask everyone to read two or three chapters of the book at home. At the next meeting, have a group discussion that involves sharing opinions or ideas about what they have read. Draw one name out of a hat prior to the meeting. This person could present a review of one of the chapters to the group.

Time

This takes a few hours over the period of your choice

Resource

Books on sales, customer service or retail topics

Benefit

- Improves specific skills
- Gives management feedback and insight into the staff's attitudes on various topics

SOURCE   Ian Low

The Perfect Pitch

What better way is there to encourage and reward positive behavior than while it is happening? This activity also gives the manager an idea of what the staff consider to be good telephone communication skills.

Purpose

- To encourage customer service and telephone sales people to use the words and the tone that will generate a positive response from customers
- To allow staff to ask for recognition and reward when they feel that it is deserved

Method

It is important that the proper use of scripts or call guides is continually reinforced. The best way to do this is while a call is happening.

Ask team members to raise a hand when they feel they are giving a 'perfect pitch' to a customer. The team leader then walks over to listen to the rest of the call. If the leader agrees that the call was good, the team member will be rewarded with a 'perfect pitch' bonus.

Reward

$10 for each pitch or $25 for five 'perfect pitches'

Benefit

- Stimulates the telephone sales and customer service staff to use professional telephone communication techniques
- Alerts the leaders to what the telephone sales and customer service staff feel is a 'perfect pitch'
- Helps in assessing who is confident and who needs more training

SOURCE   Simon Petersen

Are You Hitting the Bullseye?

This is a self-evaluation tool that will help staff members to look at their performance in a new light and encourage them to make continuous improvements.

Purpose

- To encourage staff members to think about their commitment to their position
- To improve their dedication
- To improve specific skill areas

Method

At a training session or sales meeting, ask the staff members to make a commitment to excellence—to be the best that they can be. Present a handout to them outlining the four categories described below, and ask them to discuss with another person in the group how they see themselves. In what areas of their jobs are they drifters, deciders, doers or masters? Staff could assess themselves by completing a table as shown on page 145.

Drifter: Drifts along in this area without any focus or goals.

Decider: Makes a decision to do something but never follows it through. Goals in this area become meaningless.

Doer: Faithfully does what is expected but no more. Doesn't ask the question: 'How can I improve and how can I exceed the customer's expectations?'

Master: Makes a conscious decision in these areas to be exceptional and follows through on the decision. Takes pride in making a contribution to the company and to the customer in this particular area. 'Masters' also take great pride in themselves and continuously strive for improvement.

Have a general discussion on how to become masters in all areas of the job and 'hit the bullseye'.

Staff then choose two or three skills or attitudes in which they wish to improve and they make a commitment to becoming a master in these areas. At the next meeting, team members share how they became masters in their three chosen areas.

(continued)

☞ Reproduced from *The Fun Factor: Games, sales contests and activities that make work fun and get results*
Text © 1997 Carolyn Greenwich. Design and illustration © 1997 McGraw-Hill Book Co Australia Pty Ltd

Time Two one-hour sales training meetings

Resource Handout

Benefit
- Provides an opportunity for self-evaluation
- Helps staff to set personal goals
- Encourages people to strive to improve

SOURCE Carolyn Greenwich

Trainer's Notes:

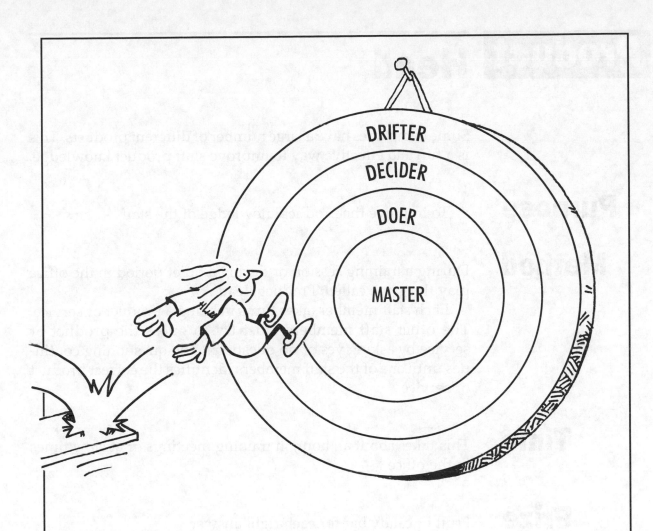

DRIFTER	DECIDER	DOER	MASTER

Product Head

Some companies have a large number of different products. This is a fun and effective way to improve staff product knowledge.

Purpose

- To improve the product knowledge of the staff

Method

During a training session or during a quiet period in the office play the game called 'Product Head'.

Each staff member takes turns in being a product or service. The other staff members must try to guess the product or service by asking yes or no questions. The questioning continues until one of the staff members identifies the correct product or service.

Time

This takes about an hour, in training meetings or at slow times in the office

Prize

Fruit or candy bar for each right answer

Benefit

- Helps staff members learn more about the products
- Creates a fun atmosphere

SOURCE   Tracy Musgrave

Trainer's Notes:

Who Am I?

Many staff need to know the different people within the organization to do their job effectively. This simple training tool works well at a large airline company to help staff learn the key names within their organization.

Purpose

- To help staff to learn the names, positions and responsibilities of people within the organization

Method

This is a guessing game that can be used to see what level of knowledge the team has about other people in the company.

Staff members form teams to compete. Information about a certain person within the organization is given to the teams in segments. The staff members are given the opportunity to guess the individual's name during or at the end of each segment of information. If they answer incorrectly, they are 'out' for that question. Continue to give information until one team gets the person's name right or until all teams are 'out'.

Sample information segments are as follows:

I have been with the company for … years.
I report to …
My middle name is …
I was born in …
I supervize … people.
My initials are …
My main responsibility is …
When you need information on … you would call my department.
My first name is …

The team that guesses the most names correctly wins.

Time

This takes about one hour

Prize

Chocolates for the team that wins most points

Benefit

- Makes learning fun and easy
- Teaches staff about people in the organization in a constructive way

SOURCE   Peter Bracewell

The T-Shirt

Are you what you wear? Ask the staff to embrace a new direction or a promotional campaign by wearing a T-shirt printed with the company slogan or campaign. Combine this with a 'jeans day' for even more fun.

Purpose

- To introduce and reinforce a new direction that the organization is taking
- To create excitement and awareness for a new product or service that the organization is introducing

Method

At the announcement of a new direction or new product or service, give each staff member a T-shirt with the message on it that is being promoted. On the day of the launch or on one day a week for the duration of the promotion, ask the staff members to wear their T-shirts to work.

Time

For the duration of the launch or promotion

Resource

T-shirts and printing

Benefit

- Builds team spirit
- Helps to change the company culture

SOURCE Rick Barrett

Trainer's Notes:

Buddy Training

This is an excellent way to develop training skills and utilize the expertise in your office. Staff members love the extra bonus. The cost to the company is minimal in comparison to other training options.

Purpose

- To involve experienced staff members in the training and development of newcomers
- To provide one-on-one 'on the job' training to newcomers
- To assist newcomers during the settling-in process

Method

Prepare a benchmark level of skills and knowledge that staff must attain to achieve Buddy Trainer status. For example, to qualify a person may need to have demonstrated or achieved the following:

1. employed for a certain length of time
2. achieved a specific inquiry to sale conversion rate
3. handled a certain number of complaints successfully
4. passed a product knowledge quiz
5. demonstrated successful customer service, telemarketing or sales results.

When they have met the criteria successfully, they then receive a certificate and the opportunity to be involved in buddy training.

The buddy training takes place as needed over half a day or one full day. The buddy trainers are given an agenda of specific skills and knowledge that they must help the trainee to achieve and implement as they sit with them throughout that day.

Buddy trainers who achieve the expected results will be asked to be involved in training again.

Time

This takes approximately half a day to one day

Resource

Clear guidelines on buddy training qualifications, certificates (see page 151) and a set of objectives and outcomes that the buddy trainer must help the trainee to achieve

(continued)

Bonus

$25 bonus for a full day, $12.50 bonus for half a day

Benefit

- Gives recognition for the talents and abilities of the buddy trainer
- Extends an opportunity to those who are motivated by extra responsibility
- Provides valuable 'how to' and 'on the job' training
- Enables the buddy trainers to become even better in their jobs—by teaching others they can also teach themselves to improve

SOURCE   Lisa Barker

Trainer's Notes:

I hereby declare
that

_____

has achieved
the dizzy heights of
qualified

BUDDY TRAINER

and is authorized to

_____

Signed _____

The Call Review

Once this activity is established as a regular feature, staff welcome the feedback. Remember to provide positive feedback as well.

Purpose

- To provide feedback to the staff on their total performance on the phone
- To encourage a higher level of customer service
- To reinforce the culture of continuous improvement of the individual and the office
- To provide a quality control measure

Method

Draw up a standard call review form, such as the form provided on page 153. The areas reviewed will be determined by the nature of the business and the type of calls.

Let the telephone sales and customer service staff know when they are being monitored, as well as how many of their calls will be monitored each week. Call reviews can be carried out by the quality assurance officer, manager, supervisor, trainer or team leader.

There may be some initial resistance to call reviewing. This can be overcome by giving lots of positive feedback about what the staff are doing right. Approach the subject of improvement areas using positive language, for example, 'In the future you will be even more effective if ... '

Time

Ongoing activity for continuous improvement

SOURCE Paul Kennedy; Janelle Nisbet

Trainer's Notes:

TELEPHONE CALL REVIEW FORM

STAFF NAME:			DATE:				

CALL REVIEWER:			TIME:				

OPENING CALL	N/A	5	4	3	2	1	0
1. Greeting							
2. Correct caller identification							
3. Procedures followed							
4. Clearly spoken language							
5. Initial rapport with customer							

DURING CALL	N/A	5	4	3	2	1	0
1. Questioning techniques							
2. Understanding of customer needs							
3. Understanding of customer's expectations							
4. Voice skills							
5. Tone							
6. Pace of voice							
7. Effective listening							
8. Helpfulness							

CUSTOMER SERVICE AND SALES SKILLS	N/A	5	4	3	2	1	0
1. Resolving problem							
2. Presenting solution							
3. Cross-selling							
4. Implementation of training techniques							

CLOSING	N/A	5	4	3	2	1	0
1. Use of trial closes							
2. Appropriate close to situation							
3. Call results							
4. Call closing salutation							

COMMENTS		/		=		%	

The Call of the Month

Make the call review (page 152) a competition that anyone can win, regardless of their experience and product knowledge. This is a great way to keep everyone on their toes.

Purpose

- To reward achievement and improvements revealed through call monitoring
- To place emphasis on the importance of each call
- To encourage people to strive for excellence during each call

Method

Explain to the team the reasons behind call monitoring. The purpose is not to catch them out doing something wrong but to help them improve their own performance.

When everyone understands the purpose of call monitoring, introduce the 'Call of the Month'. The supervisor monitors four calls per month for each person. The calls are judged according to the current experience and product knowledge of each person. This creates a fair playing field and gives everyone a chance to win. The person who achieves the best call during the monitoring period is awarded the 'Best Call of the Month'.

Time

Use this on a monthly basis

Reward

Prize selection: $50 voucher, dinner for two, time off, chocolates or wine

Benefit

- Helps to dispel the fear of call monitoring
- Gives feedback on points for improvement
- Puts focus on the importance of each call
- Enables a monthly assessment of an individual's progress
- Gives everyone an equal opportunity to win

SOURCE   Pat Caton

Share the **Laughter**

This is another training tool to help staff to understand what management means by good customer service. It also gives them ideas on how to handle specific situations that arise when dealing with customers.

Purpose

- To lighten things up
- To build camaraderie
- To reinforce positive practices
- To remind staff of inappropriate responses to customers

Method

During the week, invite staff members to write down, on colored index cards, some of the unusual comments and requests, strange questions or funny comments that customers make.

At a staff meeting, break into small groups. Give each group some of the comments by customers written down on the cards.

Ask each group to come up with responses to the following two questions for each card.

1. How would we respond if we were *not* in the business of customer service?
2. What is the best way to respond because we *are* in the business of customer service?

Share responses with the other groups to hear their reactions.

Time

One hour staff meeting

Resource

Index cards

Benefit

- Helps to relieve the stress of dealing with difficult decisions
- Helps staff to resist the temptation to 'snarl' or give inappropriate replies
- Reinforces the importance of positive customer service

SOURCE   Linda Urquhart

The Good, the Bad and the Funny

When it is time to let off steam and talk about the events of the day or the week, this activity provides a fun and easy method. Lots of material for your humor board will come out of this discussion.

Purpose

- To review the week's progress in a fun and constructive manner
- To share and learn from other staff members' successes and experiences

Method

At the weekly or monthly group or team meetings, ask the staff members to share:

1. their best success or the best thing that happened with a customer
2. the worst experience of their week with a customer and how they handled it
3. the funniest thing that happened to them.

Each person is given a three to five minute time limit to tell the group about 'The Good, the Bad and the Funny'. Encourage the team to applaud after each person's presentation as an acknowledgment of the talk.

Time

This takes about three to five minutes per person

Benefit

- Creates a positive learning environment in which staff members can learn from each other
- Gives an opportunity to tell others about some successes and funny experiences
- Allows the staff members to get some negative experiences 'off their chests'

SOURCE   Carolyn Greenwich

My week in a nutshell

The
GOOD

_____

_____

_____

_____

The
BAD

_____

_____

_____

_____

The
FUNNY

_____

_____

_____

_____

Toastmasters International

This great organization offers a wonderful development path for any company wishing to help its staff members to become more confident and to improve their communication skills.

Purpose

- To build the confidence of staff to speak in front of a group
- To improve general communication skills

Method

Contact Toastmasters International or a local Toastmasters Club (an inquiries number can be found in the telephone directory). Request some help to start a Toastmasters Club for the organization. This may start with a six to eight week Speechcraft course on your premises. These usually run for two hours once a week. The course is conducted by experienced Toastmasters from other clubs. The Speechcraft manual and other materials are provided by Toastmasters International.

During the Speechcraft course, participants learn how to give a three to five minute speech, to chair a meeting, answer impromptu questions, and improve their general communication skills. Experienced Toastmasters are invited from other clubs to speak on topics such as constructing a speech, listening, speaking with vocal variety, evaluating speeches and speaking with confidence.

At the end of the Speechcraft course, the participants have the necessary experience and knowledge to start their own Toastmasters Club with the help of the Speechcraft leaders.

Time

One to two hours per week for six to eight weeks, after or during work, for the Speechcraft course; two hours after work once every two weeks for the Toastmasters Club

Resource

Access to a training room for meetings of the Toastmasters Club after work; costs for Speechcraft course; membership fees as appropriate

Benefit

- Provides a worthwhile self-development activity at a reasonable cost
- Allows staff to gather after work in a fun and educational setting
- Gives an excellent environment for team building
- Promotes positive thinking and appreciation of colleagues
- Builds confidence and improves communication skills

SOURCE   Carolyn Greenwich

Trainer's Notes:

159

The FAIL Challenge

Making mistakes isn't stupid, but repeating them is. This on-the-job training technique will help staff members to learn from their mistakes and avoid making the same mistakes again.

Purpose

- To take away the fear of failure or of making mistakes
- To dispel the feeling of rejection in a sales or complaint handling situation
- To help staff to learn by their mistakes

Method

In a team meeting situation, explain to the staff members that no one will ever *fail* while working in the organization. This is because the word 'fail' is an acronym for '*From Action I Learn*'.

Over two to four weeks, ask staff members to record all 'fail' situations and the lessons they learned from them. At the end of this period, ask them to submit three to five 'fails' and state what lessons they learned. For each submission they receive a raffle ticket for an exciting prize.

Compile a list of all the 'fail' situations submitted and distribute it for staff members to read and vote on the top three 'fails'. To encourage voting, give each person who casts a vote a raffle ticket for an additional prize. At the next team meeting announce the top three winners, and draw the raffle for the 'fail' submissions and the raffle for voting.

Time

Hold over a two to four week period

Resource

Form for submitting 'fail' situations (see page 161), voting form, raffle tickets, gift vouchers, CDs, champagne, movie passes, lunch for two

Benefit

- Enables staff members to analyze their performance in difficult situations
- Provides a way of sharing the team's learning experiences
- Encourages staff members to turn a problem into an opportunity
- Gives an outlet to share a difficult situation by writing about it

SOURCE Carolyn Greenwich

My Three FAILS

FAIL 1 _____

From Action I Learnt _____

_____

FAIL 2 _____

_____

From Action I Learnt _____

_____

FAIL 3 _____

_____

From Action I Learnt _____

_____

Step By Step

One of the most effective ways to implement change in the workplace is to focus on one new behavior at a time. This method is a slow and steady way to effect lasting change in the workplace.

Purpose

- To change a customer service or sales behavior in an easy and non-threatening manner
- To ensure that the desired improvement is implemented

Method

Each week choose a specific behavior that would be beneficial for staff members to adopt. Explain to them that it is easier and more effective to change techniques step by step rather than in one big leap. Have a discussion with them about areas that they feel are worth improving. Hopefully they will mention areas that are also of concern to the supervisors. Decide on one behavior with which to begin. Discuss how the behavior could be improved, why it should be improved, what the benefits would be to the customer, colleagues, the company and the team members themselves. The following are examples of areas on which to focus:

1. friendly, clear greetings
2. listening more, talking less
3. using trial closes
4. asking closing questions
5. a memorable goodbye
6. cross-selling.

Practise the use of specific language through role play.

Devise a personal evaluation form, or an incentive for increased production, to encourage cooperation.

At the end of the first day, have a meeting to discuss reactions to using the new behavior. Praise the team's success and help with any problems some may be having. Ask for feedback. They may have some valuable suggestions that the team could adopt.

At the end of the week, have another meeting to give everyone a chance to discuss the outcome of the new behavior change. Ask the team members:

1. how they felt it improved their performance
2. how the customers reacted
3. what difficulties they encountered
4. why they would want to continue with the new change.

Time

One week at a time for each new behavior; continue to reinforce for two more weeks

Resource

Prompt cards for specific behavior or particular language the team members should use; materials to write in their own handwriting at team meetings

Reward

Certificates that reinforce the improvement in the behavior, for display on their desks and to act as a further reminder

Benefit

- Makes it easier and more comfortable for team members to make a positive change by focusing on one behavior each week
- Improves performance
- Increases confidence

SOURCE   Carolyn Greenwich

Trainer's Notes:

Trivia **Quiz** Party

This quiz is a great way to turn the learning of product knowledge into a fun game and a party. Staff love it!

Purpose

• To improve product knowledge in a fun and effective manner

Method

Organize a venue for a Trivia Quiz after work hours. Set the room up in team tables with three to six people at a table. Teams can be picked randomly or pre-arranged to give an even distribution of knowledge.

Develop at least ten sets of twenty questions. These should include a variety of product knowledge questions, as well as sports, current events, history, movies and any other 'trivia'.

The manager or supervisor could act as Master of Ceremonies for the Trivia Quiz party. Give the teams each set of questions one at a time. Have a time limit of five to ten minutes for the team to complete the answers. At the ring of the bell, read out the answers for the set of questions. Each team can check their own answers or the answers of the team on a neighboring table. Tally the number of correct answers for each team on a white board for everyone to see. Continue with the next set of questions.

Have a meal break halfway. Everyone could be asked to contribute to a smorgasbord. At the end of the party, award prizes for the top tables.

Time

Keep this as a regular feature

Resource

Questions, photocopies of questions, white board, tally sheet, food and beverages

Prize

First prize: $20 gift voucher for each winning team member
Second prize: Double movie passes for each runner-up
Third prize: Bottle of wine

Benefit

• Helps build team spirit and esprit de corps
• Provides a fun social activity
• Enhances product knowledge

SOURCE   Peter Bracewell

The Successful Phrase Game

This training activity will help staff to develop better communication skills. Staff members will learn to remember what particular phrases customers respond favorably to, instead of forgetting them.

Purpose

- To develop new phrases that create a positive reaction from customers
- To help staff realize the benefits of positive communication
- To share knowledge and learn from each other

Method

The team members are asked to develop new phrases or to take note of something they say that gets a positive reaction from customers. Ask them to write down these phrases during the week and describe the reaction of the customer.

At the end of a two week period, each team member should submit the phrases that they would like to share with their colleagues. For each 'successful phrase' that they submit with the response that the phrase received they are given a raffle ticket for a prize to be drawn at the end of the game.

Each contribution is added to a list of phrases for everyone to read. Each team member votes for three or five of the phrases that they like best. For voting they receive a raffle ticket for another draw.

The first, second and third place winners are announced at an appropriate forum. The raffles for submitting phrases and for voting are also drawn and announced.

Resource

Submission form for the 'successful phrase' (see page 167), raffle tickets, voting form

Time

Hold this over a two-week period

Prize

Time off, CD vouchers, gift certificates, movie passes, wine, dinner out

(continued)

Benefit

- To help people realize that selling and customer service are creative processes
- To capture for further use those phrases that are creating a favorable response from customers
- To significantly improve communication skills
- To be acknowledged by peers and management

SOURCE   Carolyn Greenwich

Trainer's Notes:

My successful phrase _____

When I used it _____

The reaction from _____
the customer: _____

_____

My successful phrase _____

When I used it _____

The reaction from _____
the customer: _____

_____

My successful phrase _____

When I used it _____

The reaction from _____
the customer: _____

The Mentor

The insurance company that has used the mentoring program is achieving wonderful results. The staff member who developed it won the 'Telemarketer of the Year for 1996' for the New South Wales chapter of the Australian Telemarketing and Call Center Association.

Purpose

- To provide staff members with the guidance, expertise and support of a mentor
- To give a resource and referral point for the protégé
- To pick up and fill any gaps in the training
- To help people achieve their personal best

Method

Establish an ongoing Mentor Program. Select from among the more experienced staff the people who:

- have a helpful and supportive manner
- possess excellent product knowledge
- set a good example
- are not team leaders or supervisors.

The mentor should guide the protégé through the following six steps:

1. techniques of harmony within the office
2. expression of pride, handling emotions and supporting team spirit
3. handling of information
4. responsibility—where it starts and where it ends
5. selective product review
6. an understanding of what staff members cannot do.

The mentor has a special relationship with a protégé which includes freedom of expression and confidentiality. There are no 'ticks and crosses', and no assessments. The protégé decides when to seek help and assistance. The mentor does not encroach on the area of influence of the team leader, senior staff member or trainer.

Time   Ongoing program to be established by management

Reward   Special recognition of the mentor and protégé relationship, such as an annual lunch

Benefit
- Adds variety and richness to the development process of the individual
- Helps a new person feel comfortable and valued within the office
- Enhances loyalty and commitment
- Adds to the effectiveness of the whole office and improves customer service and work flow

SOURCE   Anne Trouncer

Trainer's Notes:

Dispute and Distract

Not only do staff need experience, skills and knowledge to do their job well, but they also need the ability to maintain a positive mood. This is a training strategy to help them learn how to shift their mood back into a positive frame of mind.

Purpose

- To give staff members strategies for overcoming a setback
- To provide the tools for shifting from an unproductive mood into a positive mood

Method

In a group situation, ask staff members what they do to get themselves into a positive frame of mind. They will probably mention some of the following strategies:

1. take a coffee break
2. walk around the block
3. clean out desk
4. tell a joke
5. think of the 'big picture'
6. re-focus on goals
7. talk it out with a colleague
8. laugh about the difficulties.

If they mention any of the first four strategies, they are using the *distraction* technique of thinking about something else. If they mention any of the last four strategies, they are using the *dispute* technique of talking themselves out of an unproductive mood into a more positive outlook. Explain these two strategies, then brainstorm some other distraction and dispute techniques for use in the office.

Discuss the way that bad moods can affect the whole team. Everyone is responsible for the negative effect they can have on others if they do not control a bad mood. Everyone should decide on a distraction and a dispute technique that they can start using at once.

Time

Ongoing; try to come up with new strategies every few months

Benefit

- Teaches staff members how to take charge of their mood

SOURCE Carolyn Greenwich

The **Computer** Screen Saver Quiz

Successful on-the-job training techniques should make the most of all the resources at hand. For those offices where staff members have computers on their desks, this training tool is easy and very effective.

Purpose

- To use the slower periods of the day constructively
- To improve product knowledge

Method

On the computers' screen saver, compile a product knowledge quiz that changes each week. When a team member is not taking a call or attending to a customer enquiry, the screen saver will automatically appear, with questions to answer.

New questions can be organized by team leaders or by a different group of staff members each week.

At the end of each week the answers to the questions should appear. The people with the most correct answers should be acknowledged in an appropriate manner.

Time

Hold this on a weekly basis

Resource

Computers

Benefit

- Increases product knowledge
- Provides an efficient use of time

SOURCE   Shayne Everson

Trainer's Notes:

171

Survival Versus Value Culture

'You can feel it, but you can't touch it.' This is the definition of company culture by one bank's customer service center. The training discussion tool outlined below will help staff to find a way to develop and maintain a positive and productive atmosphere.

Purpose

- To create a shift in attitude
- To instil new work values

Method

During a meeting with staff members, explain what is meant by 'culture'—that it is something that we cannot see but we can feel it and experience it in an office. You may ask them to come up with a definition of culture, for example, 'the values that a group of people hold and are prepared to act on'.

Discuss differences between the two types of office culture:

1. survival based culture
2. value based culture.

Now explore the following characteristics of these two types of culture and how the staff see the culture in their office from these perspectives.

Survival based culture

(a) Approval and control are sought.
(b) Talent is more important than character.
(c) Personal agreements are more important than the big picture.
(d) 'It can't be done' is often the attitude.
(e) 'How can I be noticed?' is a question often asked.
(f) Opinions and feedback are not sought.

Value based culture

(a) Satisfaction of internal and external customers is sought.
(b) Character and talent are equally important.
(c) Alignment with company vision is valued above personal agreements.
(d) 'It can be done' is the general attitude.
(e) 'How can I make a contribution?' is a question often asked.
(f) Opinions and feedback are sought.

Have a general discussion about these points as they may relate to the department or team. Ask these questions:

1. What culture do we currently have?
2. What culture do we want?
3. How can we make a shift towards the culture we want?
4. What do we need to do now to start?

Time Ongoing during several meetings

Resource Form a 'Culture Shift' team to spearhead the new direction

Benefit
- Creates an environment of which everyone can be proud
- Improves bottom line results in the long term
- Creates a happier place to work
- Reduces staff turnover
- Makes people feel that they are valued

SOURCE Mark Stanley

My company has a strong survival ethic... You get to keep your job if you agree with the boss.

The Top Ten Excuses

Excuses, excuses, excuses—there are always excuses for disasters at the office! Meet problems head-on with this fun and effective training tool.

Purpose

- To help the sales staff overcome call reluctance and sales reluctance

Method

During a sales training meeting, discuss the personal obstacles to a sale. Form small groups and challenge each other to come up with the ten best excuses for not picking up the phone or for not focusing on the sales opportunity. Five of these can be outrageous excuses and five must be legitimate excuses (you could use the form on page 175). Here are some possible answers.

Outrageous excuses
1. Bad hair day!
2. I don't want to strain my voice.
3. The dog ate my phone.
4. Oprah's on in the staff room.
5. I might chip my fingernails.

Legitimate excuses
1. Not confident in my approach.
2. The customer might think I'm pushy.
3. They may ask me something I don't know.
4. They probably aren't in.
5. If the customers want my product, they'll call.

Each group should read out the excuses, starting with the most outrageous to generate laughter and a spirit of good fun.

Go through each of the legitimate excuses and allow everyone to make suggestions about ways to overcome call reluctance and sales reluctance.

Time

This takes about one hour during a sales training meeting

Benefit

- Helps build confidence
- Gives constructive suggestions for overcoming call reluctance and sales reluctance

SOURCE   Victor Greenwich

Top 10 EXCUSES

Outrageous excuses

1 _____

2 _____

3 _____

4 _____

5 _____

CHOMP

Legitimate excuses

1 _____

2 _____

3 _____

4 _____

5 _____

**How can we overcome the obstacles that
cause us to have phone reluctance?**

_____

_____

How Do I See Myself?

The wrong self-image can prevent some staff from doing their job to the best of their ability. As sales and customer service staff, do they see themselves as professional communicators who are providing a high level of customer service and finding solutions for the customer? Or do they see themselves in another light? This training discussion technique will help to build a positive self-image.

Purpose

- To build self-esteem
- To help staff members realize their value to themselves and to the company
- To improve customer service and sales skills

Method

Explain to staff members during a training induction or staff training meeting that their roles are as 'professional communicators' for the company.

As professional communicators, they have a great impact on how the customer views the company. When a staff member treats a call as 'just another customer' or reads from a sales script, the customer does not feel good about dealing with the person or the company.

Discuss the following three ways that they can develop as professional communicators of the company.

1. **Rapport**: How can they create a 'mini-relationship' with the customer?
2. **Impact**: How do they express what they say?
3. **Energy**: What spirit do they bring to the conversations?

Discuss how they can develop their talents further as professional communicators in these three areas. Encourage them to try out their new ideas and report back on their success in the next sales meeting.

Time

This takes about one hour

Benefit

- Stresses to staff members that customer service and sales skills are communication skills
- Helps staff members to develop their communication talents
- Improves the bottom line results
- Makes people feel valued

SOURCE Mark Stanley

Trainer's Notes:

Pass It On

Timely advice is often the best advice. This training tool taps into the experience of staff as it is gained, and provides a way to immediately share the benefit of that experience.

Purpose

- To help telephone sales and customer service people to achieve better results during a campaign
- To encourage staff to give timely advice to each other

Method

Ask each telephone sales and customer service staff member to come up with a handy hint that they can pass on to the other staff while everyone is involved in outbound or inbound calls. Provide a staff member with the 'Pass It On' handout (see page 179). The first person must come up with a piece of timely advice based on the calls that day, then pass it to the next person. Each person continues this process, adding good ideas until the whole team has contributed.

Another round of Pass It On could invite, for example:

1. words of encouragement to the other staff members
2. the best success of the day
3. a 'personal motto'
4. goals for the day.

Award a certificate or a small prize for the 'hot hint' of the day. Post all the contributions on the noticeboard or photocopy them for everyone to enjoy.

Time

Use this one day every few months

Resource

'Pass It On' handout (see page 179); certificate or small gift

Benefit

- Provides a chance to share good ideas as they occur to people during a phone or other sales campaign
- Creates a fun atmosphere
- Allows staff to communicate with peers without needless interruptions during a sales campaign

SOURCE   Carolyn Greenwich

Pass It On ...

My handy hint is:

....

....

....

Name ....

My handy hint is:

....

....

....

Name ....

My handy hint is:

....

....

....

Name ....

My handy hint is:

....

....

....

Name ....

The X Factor

Meeting customers' expectations and providing excellent customer service sometimes requires staff to be flexible and to bend the rules. Staff may worry about the risk involved by not doing things 'by the book'. But there is also a risk involved in *not* being flexible. This credit union uses the 'X Factor' as a guideline for staff when a flexible approach is required for problem solving.

Purpose

- To help staff through group discussion to develop a guideline for rule-bending and flexibility when dealing with customers

Method

Hold a group discussion with staff members to debate the factors that need to be considered when making a decision outside the normal guidelines. Discuss how to:

1. ensure that all the facts are at hand
2. assess the risk of the decision
3. consider all possible outcomes
4. consider the effect on the customer relationship.

Once the discussion is complete, ask the staff members to come up with their own guidelines called the 'X Factor', using words with 'X' in them. Provide a list of 'X' words along the following lines:

A Guideline for Rule Bending and Flexibility
Exceed customer's Expectations
Exercise discretion
Demonstrate the Exception, not the rule
Examine why things are done in a certain way
Exhaust all avenues to help the customer
Be an Expert at something
Be an Example of good service
Don't make Excuses
Excel at speed of service
Exchange pleasant greetings
Provide Exact information

Express yourself clearly
Exhibit a positive outlook
Expand on ideas
Go that *Extra* mile
Explain features and benefits
Explore problems thoroughly
Extend yourself beyond the norm
Explode after 5:00 pm.

Time

This should take about one to two hours during a sales or training meeting

Resource

Large sheets of paper and felt marker pens

Benefit

- Stimulates staff to think outside the normal procedures
- Provides staff with a sense of ownership of the guidelines they created
- Uses the 'X Factor' as an easy-reference phrase for the behavior that management would like to be reinforced

SOURCE   Chris Thiel

Trainer's Notes:

6

The **Fun** FACTOR

Recognition

The Sales Achiever of the Month

Staff will work for money and they will work for what money can buy. Sometimes what really motivates a staff member is what money can't buy. A silver trophy sitting on your desk for a month can be a powerful incentive.

Purpose

- To reward the top achiever when you do not pay commission or a bonus

Method

Each person is given a monthly target based on the territory and experience. The person who achieves the most above the target becomes the Sales Achiever of the Month.

The Sales Achiever could be awarded a large silver trophy to display in a prominent place for the month.

Time

Use this on a monthly basis

Resource

A trophy that the sales people would be proud to have on their desks

Award

Certificate for their achievements, plus a small prize, such as a book, a motivational tape or movie tickets

Benefit

- Gives recognition to the top achiever
- Gives everyone something to strive for

SOURCE   Vicki Jeffery

Trainer's Notes:

Beyond the Call of Duty

This gives you a regular procedure for rewarding and recognizing staff when they exceed expectations. Knowing that their extra effort is recognized encourages staff to go that extra mile.

Purpose

- To reward extra effort by recognition rather than money

Method

Let staff members know that the extra effort they give to their jobs is appreciated. Because everyone is so busy, it is not always possible to hear about the special contribution that some people make. Ask staff to report anything they notice that is 'above and beyond the call of duty'.

Prepare a 'Beyond the Call of Duty' certificate to present at a meeting when others are present. This gives an opportunity for people to receive verbal praise and let everyone know about their extra contribution.

Time

Ongoing reinforcement during the year

Resource

Certificates that can be printed from the computer (or use the certificate provided on page 187)

Benefit

- Helps to make the staff members feel special—everyone loves to be appreciated
- Demonstrates the attitudes that you appreciate in staff

SOURCE   Vicki Jeffery

Trainer's Notes:

Beyond the Call of Duty

In recognition
of the outstanding
contribution of

_____

who has displayed an
attitude and contribution
above and beyond
the call of duty

Signed: _____

Customer Service `Award`

A peer award is often the most valued award that can be received. This simple recognition technique is appreciated by all staff members as a chance to have their say.

Purpose

- To acknowledge and congratulate the staff member with the best customer service to both internal and external customers

Method

Each month all staff members vote for the people they feel have demonstrated the best customer service attributes in the office.

Everyone votes for three people and gives them a point score between 1 and 10, with 10 being the highest score. The person who achieves the highest number of points receives the Customer Service Award for the month.

Quarterly and annual awards can also be made to the people who have achieved the highest number of points for the period.

Time

Use this on a monthly basis, and hold quarterly and annual awards as appropriate

Resource

Plaque displayed prominently in the office with the names of winners of the Customer Service Award inscribed on it

Reward

Name on wall plaque and a gift voucher

Benefit

- Eliminates the favoritism that can sometimes appear to prejudice awards from management, as this is a peer award
- Puts focus on customer service skills and attitudes not only to customers but to each other

SOURCE   Bob Westcott

188   *Text © 1997 Carolyn Greenwich. Design and illustration © 1997 McGraw-Hill Book Co Australia Pty Ltd*

The Quarterly Awards

Why wait until the end of the year to give awards? People love recognition, so give it to them more often!

Purpose
- To bring everyone from the office or call center together for a general meeting

Method

Schedule a two-hour meeting in a venue large enough to hold everyone after hours. Make the meeting fun and positive. On the agenda, include the following.

1. Present the quarterly or annual awards for the team leader of the quarter or year, the employee of the quarter or year and the best service awards for the quarter or year.
2. Read out any bouquet letters received from customers.
3. Have a guest speaker.
4. Announce any new initiative and accomplishments.

Provide a raffle ticket for everyone who attends to go into a draw for a special prize.

Time

This takes about two hours every quarter (the staff come in their own time)

Resource

Venue and speaker, raffle tickets and prize

Award

Plaques and bonus dollars

Benefit
- Places more emphasis on the special nature of the awards
- Provides a chance to get together outside of working hours when people are not under pressure

SOURCE Jeannine Walsh

Star of the Day

This is a very timely way of giving recognition. It also provides an opportunity to say 'Every day is important'.

Purpose

• To emphasize and recognize achievement on a daily basis

Method

Each morning at the 'rev-up' meeting, target three areas that will be recognized for the day. At the end of the day, the person who is the highest achiever in the three areas becomes Star of the Day. A trophy is awarded and is displayed at this person's work station for the next day.

At the end of the week the person who has achieved the best overall results or sales achievement in each of the areas targeted for the week spins a chocolate wheel to win a prize.

Time

Ongoing on a daily and weekly basis

Resource

Trophy and chocolate wheel

Prize

Wine, dinner out, chocolates, gift certificate

Benefit

• Creates fun and excitement
• Focuses on daily achievements

SOURCE   Soula Skliros

Musical Chairs

This activity leaves no doubt in the minds of those in the office who is the top performer for that month.

Purpose
- To recognize top performance in a visual and inventive way

Method

Pick the performance that you would like to recognize for the month. It could be the same one each month or different.

In a sales team, for example, performances could be:

1. the highest sales results
2. the most improved
3. the highest conversion rate.

In a customer service team, performances could be:

1. the highest customer satisfaction rating
2. resolving the most complaints
3. best internal and external customer service, as voted by everyone in the office.

The person who wins is awarded the use of the 'very special chair' for the forthcoming month. The chair should be so exceptional that it stands out in the office or call center and gives the person who wins its use a real 'buzz'.

Time

Fun on a monthly basis

Resource

A very special chair

Reward

The use of the 'Musical Chair' for the month

Benefit
- Recognizes performance in a very visual and lasting way
- Creates some fun and good feeling

SOURCE Sally Saunders

Dragon **Dollars**

Play money that can buy goodies! This is a fun way to give continuous recognition whenever it is deserved.

Purpose

- To recognize and reward special efforts or accomplishments over a period of time

Method

Create some company or office 'dollars'. Give these dollars a special name, such as dream dollars, dandy dollars or dragon dollars. When management feels something special should be rewarded, such as an example of good service, a good call or a team contribution, the 'dollars' of various amounts can be awarded. Once a month the people who have earned the dollars can be given the opportunity to spend their dollars from a gift cupboard.

Time

Use on an ongoing basis or for one to three month periods during the year

Resource

Budget for gift items, and the company's own special dollars

Prize

A range of gift items that will appeal to the tastes and needs of the staff, such as luggage, toasters, gift vouchers or wine

Benefit

- Gives people an extra reason to provide good service or achieve sales targets
- Gives instant recognition for good work
- Creates fun, excitement and anticipation

SOURCE   Jeannine Walsh

Birthday Bashes

Birthdays are a very important day in everyone's life. Make the most of them: they are too important to overlook.

Purpose

- To celebrate the birthday of each member of the staff
- To make people feel special and remembered on their birthdays

Method

Birthdays are celebrated in a number of ways at different companies. Here are a few ideas that are easy to carry out and mean a lot to the person concerned.

1. Celebrate birthdays 'to the extreme'. Decorate the person's work station with streamers and balloons. (Vicki Jeffery, Danielle Murrie)

2. Purchase a 'designer cake' that represents some aspect of the person's interests or personality. (Vicki Jeffery)

3. Put sparklers in the cake to add a bit of fun to the celebrations. Take up a small donation from everyone to buy a cake and a small gift. (Lisa Barker)

4. Provide a funny birthday card that everyone in the office signs. (Bob Westcott)

5. Make a funny birthday hat that represents the personality or interests of the birthday person. Encourage them to wear the hat for the entire day. Take the birthday person out to lunch with you. (Alex Harper)

6. In a large office or call center choose one day in the month on which to celebrate the birthdays of everyone whose birthday falls in that month. Get together for a cake after work. (Lisa Barker)

7. Gather round the birthday person and sing 'Happy Birthday' outrageously out of tune. (Paul Kennedy)

8. Create a birthday tradition—for example, whoever is having a birthday provides the cake. (Carolyn Greenwich)

Benefit

- Makes a person feel special and lifts the spirits of other staff

The Results Board

This visual and timely tool gives ongoing recognition to the achievements of in-house sales staff. Ask the sales staff to write up their own results as they happen.

Purpose

- To display visually the ongoing results of the day for each member of the customer service or sales team

Method

Have a large white board in a prominent place that is accessible to all. On the board, list everyone's name next to particular results areas, for example:

1. appointments set
2. sales confirmed
3. calls made
4. calls taken
5. complaints resolved
6. 'hot' leads.

Where possible, give people the pleasure of writing up their own accomplishments during the day.

Reward

Recognition

Resource

Large white board and markers

Benefit

- Gives everyone a chance to measure their performance against the performance of their colleagues
- Helps to reinforce top performance
- Provides an incentive to keep figures up
- Helps management to keep track of individual and group performance as it happens

SOURCE   Simon Petersen

Best Service Luncheon

Make the most of your company board room by holding a special luncheon to recognize the achievements of staff.

Purpose

• To reward each quarter the twelve to fifteen members of the staff who have given the best service

Method

Each quarter, the winners of Best Service achievement awards can be invited to a special luncheon in the board room. In addition, eight other customer service personnel could be invited who management feels have 'gone that extra mile' in providing excellent service to both internal and external customers.

A celebrity guest, such as the managing director, could be invited. Managers could fuss over the staff by serving the lunch and pouring the beverages themselves. This always makes the staff feel special.

Time

Hold the luncheon once a quarter

Resource

Venue, food, beverages

Benefit

• Creates excitement and anticipation in the office
• Gives people something special to strive for
• Makes the best service people, who treat others well, feel special themselves

SOURCE Jeannine Walsh

The **Suggestion** Box

This is a time-tested way to get feedback. To encourage the use of the suggestion box, a reward always helps!

Purpose
- To recognize the ideas and knowledge that staff members obtain from dealing with customers every day
- To give people an opportunity to offer suggestions and feedback to management and to the teams based on their experiences
- To give people an outlet to complain in a constructive manner

Method

Provide a suggestion box and give it a special name, such as the 'What Cheezes Me Off Box'. Decorate the box in a fun way and make it a prominent feature. Next to the box, provide suggestion forms for people to fill out as follows:

1. what is the suggestion or complaint?
2. reason for the suggestion?
3. a possible solution?

At the end of each month, the suggestions are given to management to read. Any person whose suggestion is activated will be given a bonus.

Time

Make this a permanent fixture in the office

Resource

A box and forms

Reward

$20 bonus

Benefit
- Makes the most of the staff members who are in an excellent position in the 'front line' to obtain feedback and recommendations
- Gives people's comments an opportunity to be heard

SOURCE   Soula Skliros and others

Speak Out

This activity cuts right through the layers of management, so staff feel they have a direct line to the top.

Purpose

- To open the lines of communication right to the top
- To give staff members a chance to be heard in a private way

Method

Provide a 'speak out box' through which staff members can write directly to the management without consulting their immediate supervisor. They may wish to write about:

1. a complaint
2. a problem with their supervisor
3. a request for information about the company direction
4. a suggestion for improvement within the office
5. a marketing idea
6. any matter that is of concern to them.

The person writing the letter must sign it. The management reads these every two weeks. Replies are mailed to the person's home address. If staff members ask for information that the manager cannot give, then the manager tells them so and tells them why.

Time

An ongoing system that is part of the company 'culture'

Resource

A 'speak out box'

Benefit

- Gives people a chance to get things 'off their chest'
- Gives people an opportunity to take credit for their own good ideas
- Gives management a better insight into the real concerns of staff members

SOURCE Jenni Koch

Open Door Communication

To encourage communication this manager placed the staff refrigerator in his office. This ensured that everyone came into his office at least once a day!

Purpose

• To encourage freedom of speech and expression in the office

Method

Managers can indicate to people that their doors are always open to staff by:

1. keeping their doors physically open
2. moving around the office as much as possible
3. greeting each staff member personally every morning
4. discussing sensitive or personal issues in a private and supportive manner
5. encouraging people to feel free to come into their office for any reason (the staff refrigerator could be kept in the manager's office)
6. welcoming any form of feedback, good or bad, from the staff
7. watching for any barriers that might discourage open communication
8. keeping the teams small enough so there is time for communication.

Time

This management style should be established and reinforced continuously

Benefit

• Avoids having rumors spread
• Lets people get things 'off their chest'
• Gives the manager a better feeling for the 'pulse' of the office

SOURCE   Paul Kennedy

Team Leader for a Day

Trading places can be one of the best ways for management and staff to appreciate the contribution they both make. This training tool is also a fun, easy, and cost-effective competition that can boost results at the same time.

Purpose

- To reward and recognize top performance
- To help people understand the demands of another's job

Method

Choose an office deadline or a sales or customer service performance goal that you wish to reward and recognize. The person who then achieves the top performance in this designated area wins the opportunity to become Team Leader for the day.

During the following month, the team leader and the winning staff member trade places for a day. The staff member will assume full responsibility for that day—attending team leader meetings, writing daily reports and giving guidance to the other team members.

The team leader assumes full responsibility for the job of the staff member—sitting at that person's work station and handling all sales, administration or customer service duties for the day.

Time

Hold this one day a month

Reward

New responsibility

Benefit

- Helps the team leader to stay in touch with the front-line customer role
- Helps the team leader and staff member to experience first-hand the responsibilities of the other's job

SOURCE

Sally Saunders

The Newsletter

Make the most of this obvious tool! It can be fun and informative, and offers lots of opportunities for recognition.

Purpose

- To recognize the accomplishments and contributions of staff
- To set up a communication tool both for work and social activities

Method

Organize an office newsletter committee. Encourage the team to design its own newsletter format. This will probably include segments such as:

1. staff member profile
2. sales and customer service tips
3. overview from manager
4. congratulations
5. recognition
6. jokes
7. recipes
8. funny things that have happened at work
9. coming events
10. top performer announcements.

Encourage the committee to seek contributions from all staff. Mention as many people as possible in the newsletter.

Time

Make this a monthly publication

Resource

Computer, photocopier

Benefit

- Imparts useful information, sales and customer service tips and product knowledge
- Provides a tremendous way to give additional recognition
- Adds humor and general interest to the day when the newsletter is published

SOURCE   Jane Burgess; Soula Skliros

Fly a Flag

Staff at a bank customer service and sales center love this recognition method. Walking to the manager's office to pick up the flag also gives them a buzz.

Purpose

- To display the accomplishments of each employee visually

Method

Have 'flags of recognition' for each type of sale or accomplishment that the staff member makes. Every time they make a sale, reach a deadline etc., they display an appropriate flag on their work stations. Certain country flags could be used to signify certain types of sales or accomplishments.

Time

Ongoing system for displaying the staff's achievements as they occur

Reward

Flags

Benefit

- Shows everyone what each person has accomplished for the day

SOURCE   Carol York

Oscar Night

Let the imagination of the staff go wild! It is amazing how many categories you can think of when the occasion demands it.

Purpose

- To give recognition for a variety of accomplishments or contributions

Method

Organize an 'Oscar night'. As a lead up to the evening, the staff could brainstorm a variety of awards. They may come up with categories such as:

1. morale booster
2. team player
3. best listener
4. sales achiever
5. most improved
6. best sense of humor
7. best internal customer service
8. product knowledge expert.

Everyone should vote for the nominations. The three people who achieve the most votes go forward as the final nominees.

Allow a couple of weeks for lobbying to take place before the final ballot.

On the Oscar night, everyone could gather at a restaurant, dressed up as movie stars.

The Master of Ceremonies will need to have a sense of humor. He or she could comment on some of the funnier aspects of the lobbying that took place. If some funny slides of each nominee could be shown, it will also add to the fun of the evening.

The Master of Ceremonies announces the winner of each award and presents an Oscar statue.

Time

Lead up time of one month, followed by an evening out

Resource

Budget for the dinner and Oscar statues (can be purchased at most trophy stores)

Benefit

- To recognize people in a variety of ways
- To enjoy a fun evening out

SOURCE   Carolyn Greenwich

The Golden Phone Award

You do not need anything fancy for this award, just a gold-painted telephone or telephone handle. This award is highly prized by the staff at this phone center.

Purpose

- To recognize the person with the best overall results
- To tie in the quarterly bonus with monthly recognition
- To encourage excellence in a variety of areas

Method

Establish the areas on which you wish to evaluate performance. Assign a method of giving points to rate performance in each area. Areas that could be evaluated are:

1. hourly sales rate
2. conversion rate
3. amount of time on the phone
4. calls per hour
5. accuracy of input
6. call quality (as measured in The Call Review, page 152).

By including all six factors in determining the winner of the 'Golden Phone Award', a fair indication of the best overall performance will be achieved. At the end of each month, the person with the most overall points is announced as the winner. With so many elements included in the award, the competition will be closer and therefore more exciting.

Time

Hold this on a monthly basis

Reward

A Golden Phone trophy to place on the winner's desk for the month; a bottle of Scotch or wine

Benefit

- Encourages a total mix of excellence in both skills and effort
- Gives a basis for determining the quarterly bonus for all staff
- Shows staff how they compare overall with their colleagues

SOURCE Paul Kennedy

More **Recognition** Ideas

Never miss an opportunity to catch someone doing well! Outlined here are eleven more recognition ideas.

Purpose

- To show staff that their individual efforts are recognised

Method

1. At the successful completion of a three month probation period, present a small gift, such as an item with the company logo on it, to recognize the event. (Lisa Barker)

2. Celebrate a person's first year anniversary by giving a small gift at the morning tea break. (Lisa Barker)

3. Give lots of instant recognition in the form of verbal praise, such as 'I'm proud of you', 'Well done', 'Great job'. (Vicki Jeffery)

4. Make up a personalized certificate on the computer for a variety of different achievements. (Vicki Jeffery)

5. Take a different member of staff each month to an industry lunch. (Pat Caton)

6. Whenever someone volunteers for a specific task or to work late, show appreciation by buying a small, unexpected gift that means something special to that person. (Pat Caton)

7. Provide a range of special coffees and teas to show people that management think they are special. (Bob Westcott)

8. Celebrate everything! (Vicki Jeffery)

9. Recognize people's need to develop and learn by multiskilling. (Sandra Lau)

10. Stress that everyone in the office is to be recognized equally as a member of the team, all working towards a common goal, including the supervisors. Play down the 'boss' image. (Sandi Einstein)

11. Buy a bouquet of flowers to celebrate a person's first sale or first week with the company. (Carolyn Greenwich)

Twenty-one Ways to Say 'Well Done'

Sometimes offering praise is harder to say than we realize. But such an act can often make someone's day. Here are twenty-one ways to say 'Well done'.

Purpose

- To give positive verbal feedback
- To recognize performance that is often taken for granted

Method

In a busy office, it is easy to forget to pay compliments and show verbal appreciation. Here are twenty-one phrases that say 'Well done'.

1. I'm proud to have you on my team.
2. You are a bonus!
3. Congratulations on a terrific job.
4. You are so helpful. Thank you.
5. You continually improve. Well done.
6. Thanks so much for your consistent effort.
7. I really admire your perseverance.
8. Your cheerful mood lifts the spirit of the office.
9. You are a champion!
10. Wow, what a incredible accomplishment.
11. Great effort. You make us all look good.
12. I have so much confidence in you.
13. You've grasped the concept so well.
14. Your customer service skills are sensational.
15. Your sales results are outstanding.
16. Your contributions to the team are invaluable.
17. Your efforts really are making a difference.
18. You continue to delight our customers.
19. You make the company's vision come alive.
20. Your accomplishments are an inspiration to the team.
21. Customers are noticing the effort you put in.

(continued)

☞ Reproduced from *The Fun Factor: Games, sales contests and activities that make work fun and get results*
Text © 1997 Carolyn Greenwich. Design and illustration © 1997 McGraw-Hill Book Co Australia Pty Ltd

Benefit

- Makes people feel special and noticed and they respond to such verbal praise in a positive manner
- Makes people want to live up to the high expectations of them

SOURCE   Carolyn Greenwich; Victor Greenwich

Text © 1997 Carolyn Greenwich. Design and illustration © 1997 McGraw-Hill Book Co Australia Pty Ltd

List of Contributors

Christine Apoleski: Team Leader. Christine has been with St George Bank for seven years, working primarily in the telemarketing area as a telemarketing sales consultant, an assistant team leader and now as a team leader.

Bill Avery: Managing Director, Teledirect, and National Business Development Manager for the Australian Telemarketing Association. Bill is a Direct Marketing Consultant specializing in telephone sales. His major client is the Australian Telemarketing Association. Previously Bill has been a Senior Marketing Manager with Advance Bank and Hunter Douglas. He has set up two highly successful telemarketing proactive call centers. Bill was Chairperson in 1994 and 1995 for the Australian Telemarketing Association in Sydney.

Graeme Baker: Operations Manager. Graeme has been involved in telemarketing for ten years. He started as a telephone sales representative and moved into a marketing role that gave him insight into the 'how' and 'why' of telemarketing and related services. His career then progressed into telemarketing training. His current role has involved growing a call center from 11 work stations to 80, and recruiting an appropriate infrastructure of support staff to run the center.

Lisa Barker: Call Center Manager. Lisa is the manager of a newly established outbound business-to-business call center at Qantas Airways. Lisa joined Qantas to set up the operation which has grown to thirty outbound telephone account managers. Lisa's responsibility is for the motivation of the sales team and success of the center in selling to corporate clients. Previously, Lisa was Operations Manager at a 24-hour 7 days a week outsource agency specializing in the provision of customer service excellence to clients of major insurance and financial organizations. Lisa comes from a background in training and holds postgraduate qualifications in adult education. She was employed as Training Manager for the company awarded the inaugural Telstra National Customer Service Award (up to 100 employees) in 1993.

Rick Barrett: Sales Support Manager. Rick has worked in the banking industry for 17 years in branch customer service and in training. For the last three years Rick has been with Zurich Insurance in telephone sales and service management. He is responsible for teams dealing direct with customers and staff of financial institutions.

Gae Baumann: Quality Management Team Leader. Gae has been with St George Bank for over six years. Gae joined St George through a retraining scheme with Customer Vision after being out of the workforce for approximately seven years. Gae started in Customer Service in Consumer Lending and Residential Lending before becoming a Team Leader in the Quality Management area. Gae was a finalist in the Employee of the Year Awards in 1995. She enjoys all aspects of her job and is always prepared to take up a challenge.

Louise Betts: Telemarketing Consultant and Call Center Manager. For the last six years Louise has worked at all levels of telemarketing. She began as a Telephone Sales Consultant for an education company, after gaining her Bachelor of Education. Louise has worked as a Telemarketing Supervisor of a hardware and software computer company and a Call Center Manager for a health insurance company. Louise currently works as a Telemarketing Consultant, assisting companies and call centers of varying sizes with their requirements.

Kylie Black: Team Leader. Kylie has been with St George Bank for seven years and in telemarketing for two years. Kylie commenced in the service side of telemarketing for existing customers and has now moved into the sales side. For five years she worked in the branch network. The experience she gained in all different areas of the bank have been invaluable.

Peter Bracewell: Call Center Supervisor. Peter is currently Supervisor at the newly established call center at Qantas Airways specializing in outbound business-to-business telemarketing. Peter played an integral role in setting up the new operation and the design, review and ongoing development of the incentive schemes for the account managers at the center. Peter has over seven years call center experience. This includes high volume inbound at the international telephone sales center where the staff numbers exceed 250, as well as his current role. Peter's focus area is the motivation and development of call center staff. He has been involved in performance appraisal, monitoring, counseling, recruitment and training of call center staff.

Jane Burgess: Customer Service Manager. Jane has over eleven years experience in direct marketing, telemarketing and customer service in both in-house and bureau operations. Jane is now the Customer Service Manager for Nutri-Metics International in Australia. Her role involves the management and motivation of a team of customer service and telesales staff and the formulation of strategies and processes designed to bring the consumer closer to the Customer Service Department. In planning and implementing reward and recognition programs, Jane seeks the input of her team and her colleagues.

Yvonne Byrne: Customer Service Manager, Hanimex. Yvonne began her career in a customer service project management role, which led to her promotion into managing the call center for Hanimex. The call center has developed from a reactive inbound call center into a proactive outbound and inbound center. Her staff are multiskilled in both sales and customer service roles. Hanimex was a finalist in the New South Wales Chapter of the 1996 Call Center of the Year Awards. Their call center teams' motto is 'We Make It Happen'.

Luke Carey: Senior Support, Telemarketing Department. Luke has worked with the telemarketing team at Citibank since 1995. In his role as Senior Support for the telemarketing team, he enjoys bringing ideas to the team that will help build morale and keep the staff motivated. Prior to joining Citibank, Luke worked in sales and telephone sales for 12 years.

Matthew Carney: Senior Telemarketer. Matthew has worked in call center and customer service positions in the banking industry for the last seven years. He is currently with a major international investment bank.

Pat Caton: National Customer Service Team Leader. Pat joined James Hardie Building Boards in 1990 as a Customer Service Operator in a newly formed national customer service team. In 1993 Pat was promoted to Supervisor, and again in 1995 to Team Leader. Pat manages a team of twelve customer service representatives who provide technical information and handle general product inquiries and literature requests from the public and building professionals. The call center operates twelve hours a day, seven days a week.

Catherine De Vrye: Author and Professional Speaker. Catherine De Vrye is a best-selling business author and professional speaker. A winner of the Australian Executive Woman of the Year Award, her proven international management experience makes her a popular speaker in both the private and public sectors. Combining content with humor, she inspires individuals and teams on the topic 'Good Service is Good Business'; 'Conquering the Challenge of Change'; and 'Turning Obstacles to Opportunities'. Previously, Catherine was an executive with IBM, where she held roles in marketing and management development. She spent two years in Tokyo as Personnel Manager for the Asia Pacific headquarters. She also has extensive experience in the public sector.

Sandi Einstein: Call Center Manager. Sandi is currently with Link Telecommunications and has been involved with telemarketing and customer service since 1985. She was Telemarketing Manager for Imagineering, Ticketek, Drake International and Campbell's Cash & Carry. Sandi also worked with Telstra and was instrumental in the introduction of National Call and Resource Management, which used the latest technologies available internationally. Sandi is an expert in recruiting and training in all aspects of telemarketing and customer service.

Shayne Everson: Claims Specialist. Shayne moved into the 'call center world' two years ago after six years solid insurance experience. Shayne started in a customer service management role, where his duties included the establishment of call monitoring, setting service standards, as well as training and motivating staff. His current role is as the claims specialist for the call center.

Caroline Eyre: Sales Manager. Caroline commenced her career in call centers in Citibank in 1992. She has been involved in both inbound and outbound telemarketing. Currently Sales Manager at Westpac's national telemarketing center, Caroline leads a team of twelve people. The Westpac telemarketing center is committed to coaching and developing its people.

Jann Fenley: Assistant Manager, Phone Room. After 25 years in the Financial Sector, mainly involved in lending, Jann took over a telemarketing team. Jann's sales and customer service experience helped her grow a team of eight telemarketers to seventeen for the Police Credit Union. Her main challenge is to motivate her team, many of whom come from non-selling backgrounds, to achieve top sales results. Jann regularly uses a variety of competitions and visual displays of the results achieved.

Carolyn Greenwich: Keynote Speaker, Trainer and Call Center Recruiter. Carolyn Greenwich, the author, is a Director of Winning Attitudes. She specializes in the training and recruitment of both inbound and outbound telephone sales representatives, call center team leaders, and customer service personnel. Carolyn is a popular speaker and trainer. She believes in an interactive approach to training using lots of fun and motivational activities both during and after the training programs. She designs customized training programs for her clients in banking, insurance, computers, cosmetics, airlines, freight, building supplies and the travel industry. Carolyn is the Education Executive Officer for the Australian Telemarketing and Call Center Association. Carolyn and her husband Victor have been in the personnel and training field for 25 years in the United States, New Zealand and Australia. Their company, Winning Attitudes, specializes in meeting the needs of the telephone sales and call center industry.

Victor Greenwich: Director, Winning Attitudes. In addition to his extensive experience in sales, training and personnel recruitment, Victor is committed to the development of Masters Soccer in Australia and internationally, working closely with Soccer Australia. Victor is a soccer coach as well as editor of the *Soccer Coaches Journal* for the New South Wales Soccer Coaches Federation. Victor believes that the motivation of the individual or a team—whether on the sports field or in the office—is vital to the success and enjoyment of everyone involved.

Christopher Guinn: Call Center Manager. Chris began his career in customer service and telemarketing in 1976. Since then he has established many customer service centers, from small operators to major establishments. Chris is an accredited trainer, motivator and strong advocate of customer satisfaction. With his broad range of management skills he has worked as a consultant for companies who cannot budget for a full-time professional.

Alex Harper: Executive Telemarketing Manager. Alex is responsible for developing telemarketing within Rams Home Loans, a major non-bank home lender. Prior to joining Rams Home Loans, Alex was involved in branch network positions and telemarketing management for St George Bank.

Gabby Hockey: Phone Room Sales Manager. Gabby has worked within the News Limited organization for eight years. She managed and led teams in the call center environment for much of that time. Gabby believes the key areas to the success of call centers are the delivery of exceptional customer service, team effort, strong leadership and, most important of all, 'Have Fun'.

Ron James: Call Center Manager. Ron was appointed as manager to the 'greenfields' AGC Call Center site in 1993. Originally concentrated around a Predictive Dialler, the Center has expanded to handle bulk inbound and outbound traffic. Starting with two staff the center now employs in excess of 120. The core functions are collections, customer service and sales. Ron oversaw the introduction of the technology and a flexible workhour policy that allows the Center to be open longer hours utilizing a mixture of both casual and permanent staff. As a part of progressing with new ideas, self-directed teams are being trialed in one of the Center's teams. Ron's background is in the commercial sector of AGC. He recently completed his Masters in Business Management.

Vicki Jeffery: Telemarketing Manager. Vicki is currently setting up a new telemarketing department of Flick Pest Control which involves amalgamating three existing departments. Previously she set up and managed the telemarketing operation for Australia Post. Vicki is the 1996 Chairperson for the New South Wales Chapter of the Australian Telemarketing and Call Center Association. She previously served as the Events and Sponsorship Coordinator for two years.

Stephen Jones: Stephen is an experienced telephone sales representative who has worked in the publishing, financial, and telecommunications areas. He has held telemarketing and team leader roles in England and Australia and has been instrumental in creating sales competitions to create fun and achieve results.

Vasilis Karbouris: General Manager, Training. Vasilis has had a rich and diverse career in the computer industry. He is an expert at marketing computer training programs, and has worked for Ferntree, Bull Information Systems and currently for Educom Training. He joined Educom in 1990 with the task to launch and grow the training business. Vasilis uses telemarketing as one of his primary sales strategies to market training for such vendors as Novell, Microsoft and Lotus.

Elaine Karr: Supervisor, Telesales and Telemarketing. Elaine has worked in a supervisory role with QBE for the last two years. QBE telesales has both inbound sales and customer service and outbound, with inbound being the largest section. Prior to QBE, Elaine assisted the Australian Kidney Foundation in opening an outbound telemarketing operation, with the main objective to raise funds for research and to achieve a broader profile of the Kidney Foundation among the general public. Customer service excellence and staff morale have always been important issues for Elaine.

Paul Kennedy: Client Services Manager. Paul Kennedy joined Commonwealth Securities in 1995 to set up and manage Share Direct. His call center won the Australian and New South Wales Call Center of the Year Awards (for under 50 staff) in 1996. Prior to joining Commonwealth Securities, Paul was with St George Bank for 17 years. He started in a cadetship in 1979 and held several positions, including Customer Service Manager and Telemarketing Manager. In 1992 he won the Silver Management Employee of the Year Award.

Mary Kerameas: Telemarketing Manager. Mary has nine years experience in the office supply industry. For the last four years, she has managed a very successful team of twelve telemarketers. Mary uses a variety of motivation strategies that boost the morale and the results of her team.

Mike Kleviansky: Networking Consultant. Mike has spent two years as Education Service Business Manager for a major network distribution company. During this time, he was responsible for the training budget and frequently used 'fun' selling techniques to motivate staff in an effort to achieve budget.

Jenni Koch: Manager of NSW TAB telephone and computer account betting operation. Jenni is responsible for a large call center spanning three sites, with 650 seats, over 900 staff, a call answering rate of 15 million annually, with a call duration of 45 seconds, and an abandonment rate of less than 1%. Previously, Jenni had a successful career in software development and telecommunications management. Her previous employers include IBM Australia and the Commonwealth Bank of Australia.

Sandra Lau: Call Center and Customer Service Manager. Sandra has been with *Sydney Morning Herald* Classifieds section since 1978. She started as a Telephone Sales Adviser in an incoming telephone room. Since that time Sandra has been involved in training and supervising the telephone staff. In 1992, she took on the challenging role of Call Center and Customer Service Manager of 120 staff. Recent challenges have been the relocation of premises without interruption to business and the transformation from a totally inbound to a mix of inbound and outbound advertising services with a high emphasis on customer service. Sandra finds the call center an ever changing, exciting and evolving environment in which to work.

Ian Low: Business Development Manager for Sales Pursuit Seminars. Sales Pursuit brings leading speakers from a range of countries to the Australian marketplace in the area of sales training, management and personal development. Ian has been in the forefront of the company's sales success for the last four years, developing and implementing highly successful telephone sales campaigns. He currently heads up the Anthony Robbins division of the company.

Anne McFadzean: Business Development Manager. Anne is a specialist in the promotion of general insurance products through credit unions. Since 1984, her expertise has been honed through positions with insurance companies, credit unions and recently the Credit Union Services Corporation, the movement's peak body. Her current role is to assist 244 credit unions take a committed approach to developing and growing their insurance business. A key component in Anne's roles has been to maintain motivation, notably as Insurance Manager for a large credit union, where she instigated programs to assist staff in seventeen branches to actively and enthusiastically promote insurance among a myriad of other financial products.

Muffy McWhinnie: Corporate Trainer with Power Performance Management Training. Muffy received her Master's degree in Performing Arts from UCLA in 1972, followed by involvement in television and theatre dance productions in Los Angeles and Las Vegas. Muffy's experiences also include working as a telephone complaints manager for a leading plastics company and running her own manufacturing company. She now combines her business experience and knowledge of performance psychology as a complaints management and presentation skills trainer. She believes that the 'dance' between the customer and the staff is a special performance of its own, requiring well rehearsed steps to consistently ensure positive results.

Danielle Murrie: Client Services Manager. Danielle works for the Australian Guarantee Corporation. She established an outbound sales and proactive service team within the retail funding, consumer division. The aim is to provide excellence in customer service whilst meeting sales targets. Previously, Danielle established the first outbound telemarketing sales unit for Cigna Insurance Australia. Danielle is a marketing graduate of the University of New South Wales.

215

Tracy Musgrave: Customer Service Center Manager. Tracy has an extensive banking background. While most of her experience has been in lending, she has had the opportunity to work in a number of branches and departments of the Commonwealth Bank of Australia. Her years in the customer service center have been challenging and rewarding. Being able to assist customers and to work with energized staff is a major 'positive' of each working day. The ability to focus on staff coaching and up-skilling and to see a real value-based culture take shape is thrilling and rewarding.

Janelle Nisbet: Call Center Operations Manager. Janelle works for Commonwealth Securities Ltd. Janelle was hired as a Team Manager in 1995 to help set up Share Direct by assisting in the recruitment, training and development procedures and to help establish the culture. Currently Janelle's role is to manage quality control by call reviewing, coaching and looking for ways to improve. Her previous background is in training and development in the banking industry.

Nina Pennisi: Business and Development Manager. Nina has worked with St George Direct for thirteen years. For the first seven years, she worked in the branch network and moved up to branch management level. Six years ago she moved to the head office to become involved in telemarketing. While her face-to-face selling experience had been challenging and exciting, it was nothing compared with the new venture of telemarketing. Nina has worked as both a service and sales consultant and supervisor before becoming Business and Development Manager.

Sandy Perrett: Sales Trainer. Sandy has more than nine years experience in managing, owning and consulting for call centers in the US, the UK and in Australia. Sandy holds a Bachelor of Economics. He provides all of his clients with a money-back guarantee if they do not improve their sales results after his training.

Simon Petersen: Managing Director, Instant Office Supplies. Simon started in telemarketing in 1972. For twenty years he has managed teams of thirty telemarketers in the stationery supply business.

Judy Purdon: Cross Marketing Manager. Judy has more than fourteen years experience with very successful results as a Sales Executive, Telemarketing Manager and Sales Recruiter and Trainer. She has managed sales and customer service people in insurance, cosmetics, car rental and telemarketing bureau industries. At MMI Insurance she put in place a very successful 12-hour, seven day a week roster and introduced telecommuting. With Avon she set up the telemarketing department that grew from four to forty staff. With Avis she set up training and recruitment programs that achieved a significant improvement in workforce morale and stability.

Bill St James: Direct Marketing Manager, Australian Kidney Foundation. Bill joined the Kidney Foundation in 1994 to implement a telemarketing center to raise funds. Since its beginning, the telemarketing center has achieved tremendous success raising funds through Bill's innovative approaches and determination. Prior to joining the Kidney Foundation, Bill established a Financial Services Business utilitizing telemarketing to great success and profit. Bill's background also involves extensive experience at top levels in the Tourism and Hospitality industry.

Sally Saunders: Call Center Consultant with Coolong Consulting in Australia. Sally Saunders has worked with leading American and Australian organizations to create, develop, and improve call centers since the mid 1970s, and as a consultant since 1984. Today, Sally lives in Australia where she leads a team of professionals who consult on all aspects of telephone-based operations — strategic planning, management, operations, process engineering, telephone and information systems. Her own expertise focuses on the issues related to planning, management and the development and motivation of staff.

Nada Simovski: Business and Development Manager. During Nada's eight years with St George Bank, she has been involved in telemarketing. Nada began as a Telemarketing Sales Consultant, progressed to Team Leader and now holds the position of Business and Development Officer in the sales environment.

217

Lavina Siumaka: Staff Lending Officer. Lavina has been with St George Bank for eight years. The majority of that time has been spent in residential lending. Currently as the Staff Lending Officer, Lavina provides service to the staff of the bank on secured and unsecured loans, and comprehensive insurance products. She also assists and processes savings and overseas transactions.

Soula Skliros: Telemarketing Manager. Soula has been working in telemarketing for seven years. Soula joined Citibank in 1995 to set up and manage the National Telemarketing Center to fulfil both inbound and outbound telesales functions. The center has achieved early successes and continues to grow as a very effective sales channel. Prior to joining Citibank, Soula managed a team of inbound and outbound telesales representatives for a health fund. Soula has herself worked as a Telephone Sales Representative generating insurance leads for the sales forces. Soula has a Bachelor of Arts degree and a Diploma of Education, majoring in legal studies.

Mark Stanley: Chief Manager, Customer Service Centers. Mark has been responsible for the development and operation of the Commonwealth Bank of Australia's teleservicing and telemarketing capability in Sydney, Melbourne and Brisbane, which involves over 800 staff. Prior to this, Mark was the start-up Center Manager for the Sydney Customer Service Center. Practical experience was supported by exposure to call center practices in Britain while occupying the role of the European Representative for the Commonwealth Bank of Australia in the early 1990s. Mark has recently completed postgraduate studies in Finance and Marketing at Macquarie University's Graduate School of Management. These studies have further added to his understanding of the complexities and breadth of issues involved in leading a team in the call center distribution option.

Jenni Swistak: National Telemarketing Manager. Jenni has been involved in telemarketing and telesales since 1987. As the National Telemarketing Manager for DHL International (Australia) Pty Ltd, Jenni was responsible for setting up and running the national telesales unit based in Melbourne. The DHL telemarketing center has won the Call Center of the Year

Award in Victoria for the last two years. Jenni has a Bachelor of Business degree in Marketing and Organizational Behavior. Over the past nine years, Jenni has managed both inbound and outbound call centers in the computer, health, telecommunications and transport areas. Jenni initiated the establishment of a South-East Asia Telesales User Group for DHL International. She established a best demonstrated practice throughout the extensive network of call centers within the South-East Asia region of DHL International. Jenni is also a regular speaker at conferences and workshops on call center issues and development.

Chris Thiel: Assistant General Manager of NT Credit Society, the largest locally owned credit union in Australia's Northern Territory. Prior to this appointment, Chris also held the positions of Corporate Development Manager and Marketing Manager. In each role, she has been involved with organizational strategy and planning and has been responsible for customer service and sales strategies. Chris has developed and implemented customer service standards, sales and service training, and service quality monitoring systems across a range of distribution channels, including traditional branches, new personal financial centers, call centers and automated electronic and IVR services. Creating a happy marriage between 'high touch' and 'high tech' is seen by Chris as an important challenge and her organization has earned an enviable reputation in the market for this accomplishment.

Anne Trouncer: Mentor. Anne returned to the workforce in 1991, joining Zurich Insurance as a Sales Consultant. Her enthusiasm for sales grew as she learned to discern the client's real need and acquire the self-discipline to address that need. She moved into the outbound service role, before setting up the Mentor Program where Anne works as a full-time Mentor. Her task is to 'grow' the individual for the benefit of the team, to assist in developing latent talent and ability and to reveal to the team member the underlying worth of the daily task. Anne is also a chartered librarian.

Linda Urquhart: Keynote Speaker and Trainer. Linda develops customized training for local, regional and international clients in the areas of leadership, team building, strategic planning, communications, personality styles and board development. Linda motivates, entertains and educates her audience. Her unique style as a presenter, facilitator and trainer incorporates active, fast-paced and hands-on learning experiences. Based in Spokane, Washington, Linda has held key roles in the community and State as President of the Pacific Region for the National School Boards Association, the Washington State School Board's Directors Association and the Spokane School Board. Linda holds a Masters degree in Education from Stanford University. Linda can be reached through Winning Attitudes, Spokane, Washington.

Jeannine Walsh: Chief Manager, Direct Delivery St George Bank. Jeannine's career in telemarketing spans over eight years. Previously Jeannine held various management positions within St George Bank over a twenty-eight year period. Jeannine established St George Direct in 1980 which is recognized as a leader in telemarketing and customer service within the financial sector of Australia. St George Bank won the 1995 National Award for the Best Call Center of the Year. Jeannine is a founding member of the Australian Telemarketing and Call Center Association. She is past President and Vice-president, currently holding the position of Sponsorship and Events Coordinator. Jeannine is a regular speaker at both local and national conferences on a range of issues associated with doing business via the phone and customer service.

Bob Westcott: Manager, Telesales and Telemarketing. Bob began his career in telemarketing in 1985 when he was given the task by his employer, the State Bank, to establish a 24-hour call center operation. Bob developed the operation to a full sales and service function. 1n 1991 he joined QBE Insurance to establish a full sales and service center. He continues to develop and enhance the operation. Bob was the original founding member and President of the Australian Telemarketing and Call Center Association. He is currently serving a second term and looking forward to continuing to promote and push the industry forward through the Association.

Kaye Wetzler: General Manager, Credit Union. Kaye has worked for twenty-four years in the Credit Union industry, and twenty years in management. She is a member of the Australian Institute of Credit Union Management and a 'Dude' Down Under Development Educator. This involves assisting emerging Credit Unions in the South Pacific and South-East Asia through skills transfer. Her biggest 'buzz' is helping someone within her team to surpass their potential. Her goal is to have the team members understand that motivation comes from within themselves and from working in an organization whose values align with theirs.

Susan Williams: General Manager, Customized Services, Manpower. Susan has been involved in telemarketing and telesales since the mid 1970s. Susan has held various senior management positions, including General Manager in the call center, personnel, sales, and wholesale and manufacturing industries. She has been directly responsible for the recruitment, training and management of workforces ranging from 40 to 260 people during her career. Currently as the General Manager of Customized Services for Manpower, she helps to innovate staffing strategies with large organizations, outside the traditional form of permanent and temporary recruitment. Susan is a member of the National Executive Committee for the Australian Telemarketing Association and an active speaker at conferences and seminars. Her reputation has been built on the success of her visions and strategic management efforts.

Trevor Williams: Call Center Manager. Trevor works for the Commonwealth Bank of Australia. As a career banker, Trevor has been exposed to virtually every facet of banking. He has worked throughout Australia, Papua New Guinea and the Solomon Islands. Trevor has a diverse range of expertise, mainly in the area of training and development, human resources and general operations involving large groups. In 1993, Trevor was involved in setting up the Melbourne call center and together with his management team developed a highly productive environment with a strong emphasis on ownership at all levels. With a clear focus on results, team leaders have developed a 'fun' culture in which teams employ a wide variety of games to assist them in achieving high lead generation levels.

Carol York: Banker and Call Center Manager. Carol's career spans twenty years in the banking industry. Her roles have included National Telemarketing Manager, Project Manager, Operations Manager, Customer Service Manager and Training Manager. Carol has worked for Westpac Banking Corporation, the State Bank of New South Wales and NatWest.

Wayne Lewin: Team Leader Commonwealth Bank of Australia Call Center. Wayne has worked for the bank for over 11 years within the branch network. Wayne was one of the initial Sales and Service Representatives when the bank opened its Customer Service Call Center. Since being promoted to a Team Leader, Wayne has developed a variety of games to help the staff achieve a higher level of performance. He believes 'Fun' is a great way to motivate the team. Wayne's Football Match Game has been used successfully in the Bank's other Call Centers with great results.